Copyright © 2014 by Tracey Webb and Richard Mowbray. 603183
Library of Congress Control Number: 2014914116
ISBN: Softcover   978-1-4990-8845-8
         Hardcover   978-1-4990-8847-2
         EBook   978-1-4990-8846-5

Rev. date: 11/17/2014

To order additional copies of this book, contact:
Xlibris
0-800-056-3182
www.xlibrispublishing.co.uk
Orders@ Xlibrispublishing.co.uk

GREAT!

YOU MADE IT!

We want you to be inspired & creative, but above all, we want you to have fun with this book!
Our aim is to make vegetarian, vegan, raw & gluten-free diets easy going, with lip-smacking recipes!
This book is designed to help you achieve a level of good health & energy without having to take large daunting steps, or eating tasteless foods.

We will look at many different types of food, from raw to roasted to sprouting, from different parts of the world & what these foods can do for you on a nutritional level.
There is something for everybody in this book & we hope you enjoy the recipes, information & the tips within.
If you don`t have the exact ingredient to hand, don`t worry we encourage you to be creative, so we have made some suggestions to help you get around this.

There is no easy way to explain in a nutshell what this book is actually about, apart from good food, good vibes &, our ethos!

We sing & dance in the kitchen every single day! Richard will whip-out his pro drumsticks & bang out a solo on the pans, bowls, the lemon juicer, or whatever else is within arm's reach.
We believe that laughter & positive energy are so very important to preparing delicious food!
As a result of which the laughter emanating from our kitchen is often audible to all!
Again, we want you to have fun with this book :)

We hope that you enjoy prepping & cooking with us!

THIS IS NOT JUST A RECIPE BOOK

It is also a manual for healthy living where you will learn about; the benefits of herbs & spices - raw vs. cooked – chlorophyll – blood ph. –enzymes – fats – sprouting - & more!

ॐ   Raw vs. cooked

ॐ   Organic vs. commercial (photo of kirlian mushroom)

ॐ   The importance of blood ph & what foods are acidifying &alkalizing

ॐ   The importance of chlorophyll

ॐ   What are Enzymes & why are they so important

ॐ   How to sprout & grow your indoor greens

ॐ   Home remedies

ॐ   Good fats bad fats

ॐ   How to make nut milks & creams

ॐ   Some myths broken!

ॐ   And for you non-believers a list of pertinent reading material at the end of this book which are packed with case studies.

   Oh yes, & the recipes themselves!

CONTENTS

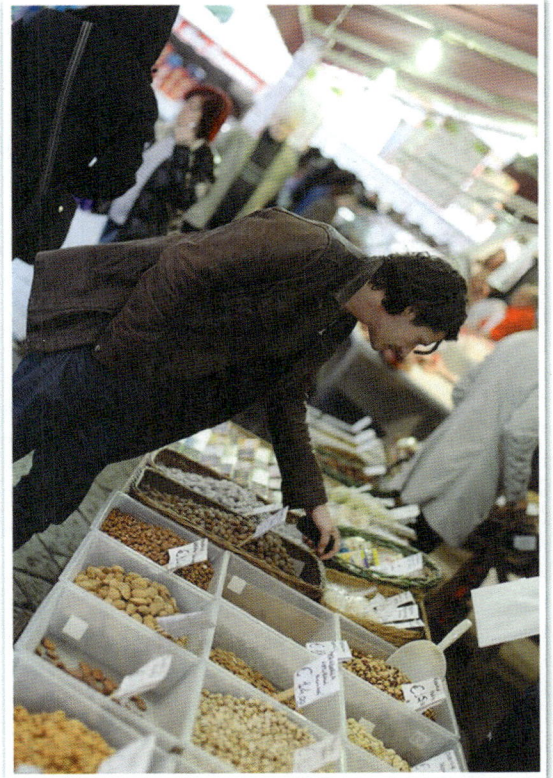

V   **Veggie-Vegan**
All our recipes are vegetarian.
In dishes that contain dairy products
we have suggested a substitute
ingredient to"Veganise" them

R   **Raw**
These recipes are primarily vegan,
& are never heated above 40°c (104°f)

RC   **Raw with Cooked Elements**
As discussed in "cooked versus
raw" we have prepared
some recipes that contain cooked
elements

GF   **Gluten Free**
Although we do use grains containing
gluten, we provide you with an
alternative ingredient

OUR TERMINOLOGY:

When we say "Olive oil" or extra virgin olive oil)

We are referring to a good quality "extra virgin olive oil" Extra virgin referring to the first cold press! You can find an array of olive oils in the shops. I would recommend you buy a "suave" soft light olive oil for cooking. The more intense flavours are excellent for salad dressings, etc. Please use which ever oil suits your tastes, be it sesame, coconut, etc. However be aware that corn, & vegetable oils are nasty. Refer to info at the back of the book.

When we say "salt"

We are referring to Himalayan salt, it is said to be the purest salt on earth & it also contains all of the elements (this salt has well over 70) found in your body. The table salt of today is cooked, along with its caking agents at over 1200 degrees altering the molecular structure. This salt is 250 million years old! If not a good quality sea salt such as Maldon is a fine replacement.

When we say "syrup or sweeteners"

Use whichever element suits your body, be it palm sugar, stevia, honey, raw un-processed organic sugar, please see info on Sugars at the back of the book.

When we say "tamari"

You can use tamari or a good soy sauce

MORE INFO!

YOU WILL FIND HEAPS MORE INFORMATION AT THE REAR OF THIS BOOK; HOWEVER FOR NOW

LET'S GET CRACKING!

COOKED VS RAW

Definition of raw food: a food that still has its enzymes intact.
Things that happen when we cook a food:
Vitamins are denatured & rendered practically useless
Around 50 % of protein is denatured
The Enzymes within die (Enzymes are made from protein) starting at 40°c/105°f
However we retain the minerals

I believe we started off as raw foodies, then, as we mastered fire we discovered that food tasted better when cooked, maybe cave people had enough of eating raw during the winter! Or maybe we were all on the same mega continent (Pangea) around the equator & never had winter & so we always ate raw! I don't know, but what I do know is nowadays we cook practically everything, our enzyme reserves are depleted (please see info on Enzymes) we are constantly wasting energy in the digestion of nutrition-deficient food, we don't drink enough water, we don't exercise & our diets are acidic. Fact is there is a case of global mal nutrition going on, obese or not, it doesn't matter, just because we "look good" on the outside it does not mean everything is good on the inside.
Raw food is a good way to give the body a break from wasting of energy.
I am not going to stress you out & say go 100% raw, it is not necessary, let me explain. In the 1930's nominated Nobel-prize candidate Dr Kauchakoff ran a series of experiments regarding cooked vs. raw: in a nutshell, he found that when we eat 51 percent cooked the body goes into "digestive leukocytosis" (the activation of white blood cells) which means the body still recognises cooked food as a foreign invader. It suggests however that we have evolved about half way to adapting to an all cooked food diet. This means you don't have to go bonkers & go 100 % percent raw but if you could do say 55 % that would be very beneficial for you. As for measuring what would be a 49/51 percent ratio on your dinner plate? I don't know!
This is what I would do:
For breakfast I would have a nice organic juice, some raw muesli with freshly made almond milk, goji berries, some raw cacao nibs & with chopped fruit on top. That is all raw. If you like toast then maybe try & substitute butter with olive oil or a nut butter & maybe an avocado on top, or as they do here in Spain, grated tomato.
Even if you don't like raw muesli & prefer the "dead" variety you still have the raw extras & toppings to add to it. I would make the mix around 50 50.
If you are a meat eater (one of the most difficult foods to digest unless it is raw,) then have your steak but have a large salad, not chips as this is the worst thing you can do for digestion, mixing proteins & carbs. Choose one of the raw desserts in this book, & then you will have had at least some raw, maybe not 50 percent but not 100 percent cooked either. If you have & or like pineapple have a few chunks 15 minutes before your steak, pineapple has a digestive enzyme call Bromelain which digests protein, so this will start the process of digesting your meat before your body starts using its enzymes. (Law of adaptive secretion E Howell)

ORGANIC VS COMMERCIAL

Why do we have commercial production? It is an easy way of mass producing cheaply whilst at the same time making more money for the shareholder & the company.

The 3 main nutrients used in modern farming mass production methods are nitrogen, phosphorous & potassium, but in fact a good healthy soil will need at least 52 different minerals to give proper nutrition to the growing plant, (we are comprised of 6 main elements & around 23 trace elements). What plants actually do is to draw up all the inorganic mineral & through photosynthesis transform them into organic minerals, a form which the body can absorb very easily.

No wonder we have to throw all these chemical pesticides & fungicides on the land, because the plant growing in this nutrition-deficient land will never have the capacity to defend itself due to the lack of essential minerals in the ground. Some of these minerals are trace minerals but important nevertheless to the overall balance & health of the organism.

We are the same; we are deficient in many different nutrients so instead of ingesting fungicides & pesticides (like the plants) we take pharmaceuticals! If we have proper nutrition then our bodies & minds will be in a much better position to heal. One way of doing this is to eat organic whenever possible, you would be cutting out all the toxins from the various synthetic chemicals, toxins that can stay in your body for many years, or even all of your life unless you detox from time to time. Another point is that your body will not absorb all the nutrients from a commercially grown food (only about 50 % of the nutrients get absorbed & used). Another thing to mention is that the majority of the nutrition lies in the skin of the fruit or veg so it does make sense to eat organic produce.

If money is tight, then a cheap way of doing this is to buy enough organic fruit & veg for a juice or two a day, then at least then you can drink & absorb its nutrients without wasting any, which we tend to do because generally we don't chew our food properly & therefore we don't digest properly.

One last consideration is that our food, both organically & commercially grown, travels at least 1 week before hitting the supermarkets. Farmers markets for me are the best way to buy; hopefully you have one near you. If you have the time & space, you can always grow your own.

A tip on detoxing can be found at the rear of this book.

WHEN YOU EAT AN ORGANIC, NON-COOKED PIECE OF FRUIT OR VEGETABLE, YOU ARE EATING THE LIGHT OR LIFE FORCE OF THE PLANT

Aura Energy photography, you can see the life energy (in green) omitted in the photos below

Non-organic | Organically grown

Non-Organic Basil
Commercially Grown

Organic Basil

OUR PASSION
RICHARD MOWBRAY

My first glimpse into cooking was at the age of six (back in the 70's,) in Italy, I used to hang out in the kitchen with my grandmother keenly watching what she was doing, asking her questions & of course being there as "quality control", as a taster!

In my teens we had a communal kitchen at school which is where I started cooking for my friends & I in self-defence (because school food was so yummy - YUK!) & this spurred me on to take cooking lessons at the school. The fact that I had control of the final taste of the dish I was preparing was so interesting that I would frequently try out new flavours & change the recipes, sometimes it worked, sometimes it didn't. It was such fun!

The next twenty years I would be on a diet of meat, dairy, & processed foods... needless to say I started piling on the pounds. I thought it was normal as this is what everybody else was doing & so no one really gave it any thought that our life styles at the time, including our diets, could be the major contributing factor to many of the conditions we had. Furthermore any ailment we did have was referred to the Doctors who then would prescribe a pill... It was Betty, co-founder with me of Centro Punto de Luz, who whilst studying at the Institute of Optimum Nutrition introduced me to the "crazy idea" that foods, if consumed correctly & in the right state, had the power to reverse many conditions we see today. The penny dropped & I got hooked. I was never one to go & study a whole 4 year degree on the subject; I did however send myself on many courses & read a lot on the subject & learned how different food groups do different things for the body & mind. I figured instead of taking pharmaceuticals why not take the plant version instead? There it was; a way of healing the body with no side effects, amazing! I mean it was Hippocrates who said 430 BC "Let food be thy medicine & medicine be thy food". He was spot on!

In my 30's Betty & I had decided to leave the UK & move to Spain with a view of opening up a retreat, which we did in 2009 & we called it Centro Punto de Luz, or Source of Light. This was the perfect vehicle to be able to further my work on food & nutrition as I would be running the kitchen & preparing all the meals together with Tracey. This is where my main culinary journey began. I worked out that you could have your cake & eat it, that you could still make tasty delicious food without compromising your health. This is not a book on extreme diets; it is neither a book which is trying to force you to do something you don't want to do. It is designed to be a book for everyone, a book with a bit of everything in, something for everyone; it is book which replaces unhealthy ingredients with healthy ones. Although we have kept some unhealthy ingredients too, you will be able to swap these out if you wish. Remember, it is what you do every day that counts.

OUR PASSION
TRACEY WEBB

Known as Nell; I started cooking at a very early age, where I both assisted & hindered my grandmother in the kitchen. I started cookery classes at the age of twelve; to my mother's delight I was really good at it! Over the next few months we came to an unspoken arrangement, I would cook, & Mum would clean-up. Everyone was happy.

I took my first step to becoming a vegetarian at the age of ten, five years later; I stopped eating meat & fish all together. I moved to Spain many years ago, & I have spent a lot of time in Morocco over the last twenty years; cooking with my friends in their homes, this is where you find authentic local delights. It's difficult not to be inspired by the range of fresh organic ingredients that the ladies bring to sell in the villages on a daily basis.

One of my passions is teaching people to cook, another is photography. So when the opportunity arose to write a recipe book, this offered me the possibility to incorporate both interests. My aim is to enlighten people to the fact that eating & preparing healthy food, can be easy & fun! Very often recipe books are far too formal. I wanted to write a recipe book that was a lot more relaxed. We want to simplify our recipes as much as possible, & encourage our readers to experiment, instead of getting stressed in the kitchen.

I experiment in my kitchen on an almost daily basis, & love entertaining friends, half of whom are vegetarians. I am constantly infusing different flavours from various fresh herbs, spices & citrus or tropical fruits. I love to bake bread, cakes & cookies, as well as creating exceptional salads! Many friends' have requested that I open a restaurant locally, or write a cookery book; I'm not interested in opening a restaurant, so here is the book guys…

The last few years I have been teaching cookery workshops, raw, vegetarian & vegan food, which have proved popular. I teach people practical hands-on cooking techniques. So I invite them into my home & show my clients that making pasta dough is a fun experience, not an overwhelming one. Then we sit & share the meal that we have prepared together. The reward being the emails that I receive thanking me for giving them the confidence to remove the pasta machine from the box & successfully make their own home-made pasta!

I started working as a raw chef when I was approached by Richard to work alongside him at the yoga centre Centro Punto da Luz. Upon our first meeting, both our food ethics & our positive energy matched. Since then we have become good friends & have been creating tasty infusions of flavours ever since!

Enjoy! ॐ

CENTRO PUNTO DE LUZ
ACKNOWLEDGEMENTS

BETTY &RICHARD FOUNDED "SOURCE OF LIGHT" AS IT IS KNOWN BY OUR MANY GUESTS. IN NOVEMBER 2009 WE REALLY DID NOT KNOW WHAT LAY AHEAD AS WE NERVOUSLY AWAITED OUR FIRST GUESTS IN THE SUMMER OF 2010, WE SOON FOUND OUT...

THE MAIN MISSION, APART FROM CREATING A GREAT VENUE IN A STUNNING LOCATION, WAS TO PRODUCE THE KIND OF FOOD THAT WOULD RESTORE & RE-ENERGISE OUR GUESTS DURING THEIR STAY WITH US. TO SHOW THEM THE REAL POWER OF PROPER NUTRITION WITHOUT HAVING TO SACRIFICE THE FLAVOURS WE SO LOVE TODAY, TO TAKE OUT THE BAD INGREDIENTS & REPLACE THEM WITH HEALTHY ONES.

THE FORMULA OF PART RAW & PART COOKED WAS A COMPLETE SUCCESS & SO WHEN TRACEY JOINED US IN 2012 AS SOUS CHEF WE BEGAN OUR JOURNEY TO WRITE THIS BOOK.

THERE ARE MANY PEOPLE I WOULD REALLY LIKE TO THANK & YOU KNOW WHO YOU ARE BUT IN PARTICULAR BETTY FAVOT, WHO HAS BEEN INSTRUMENTAL THROUGHOUT THE "CENTRO PUNTO DE LUZ PROJECT". ELAINE BRUCE (UK CENTRE FOR LIVING FOODS) WHO EXPANDED MY KNOWLEDGE ON LIVING & RAW FOODS & OF COURSE MY CLOSE FRIEND TRACEY, WITHOUT WHOM I WOULD NOT HAVE BEEN ABLE TO GET THIS BOOK WRITTEN AT ALL!

THANK YOU. THANK YOU. THANK YOU.

TRACEY'S ACKNOWLEDGEMENTS

THANK YOU UNIVERSE! LET THE LOVE FLOW

I WOULD LIKE TO GIVE THANKS TO MY AMAZING HUSBAND STEVE FOR HIS INVALUABLE GUIDANCE & ADVICE REGARDING CREATIVE DESIGN. THANK YOU FOR YOUR PATIENCE & KEEPING ME GROUNDED THROUGHOUT THE PROCESS OF WRITING THIS BOOK. NOT TO MENTION CHIEF TASTE TESTER OVER THE LAST TWENTY-FIVE YEARS! LOVE YOU...

I WOULD ESPECIALLY LIKE TO THANK MY FATHER, DAVID GOZNA, FOR HIS REMARKABLE PHOTOGRAPHIC SKILLS. THANKS FOR FLYING TO MALAGA TO COMPOSE SUCH STUNNING PHOTOS, MAKING OUR BOOK TOP-NOTCH! LOVE YOU PAPA BEAR.

THANK YOU RICHARD & BETTY FOR CREATING & SHARING SUCH A BEAUTIFUL ENVIRONMENT & PROVIDING A RELAXED ATMOSPHERE FOR MANY PEOPLE TO ENJOY. IT IS A PLEASURE TO WORK IN SUCH A PEACEFUL RETREAT, WHERE I AM APPRECIATED & TRUSTED, ALLOWING ME TO BE CREATIVE IN THE KITCHEN. I AM GRATEFUL FOR THE FACT THAT WE HAVE BECOME FAMILY. LOVE YOU GUYS!

THANK YOU TO OUR GRAMMATICAL EDITORS, & GOOD FRIENDS MARK & SARAH. WITHOUT THEM, THIS BOOK MAY HAVE BEEN COMPLETELY ILLEGIBLE!

I WOULD ALSO LIKE TO DEDICATE THIS BOOK TO OUR BEAUTIFUL BROTHER & SISTER, OUR BEST FRIENDS SVEN & BRITTA. BRITTA WAS AN EXCELLENT COOK. OVER THE YEARS WE SPENT MANY HOURS LAUGHING & EXPERIMENTING IN THE KITCHEN. BRITTA WAS PURE SUNSHINE IN OUR LIVES & WILL REMAIN FOREVER IN OUR HEARTS ॐ

ETERNALLY THANKFUL TO MY FUN-LOVING MUM GLORIA

EQUIPMENT

Apart from the norm, we have a few main pieces of equipment we use. You may find these items are a little on the expensive side, however you are making an investment in your health.

THE THERMOMIX TM31: This is an expensive machine we use here, however it's well worth the investment if you can afford it. These machines are made in Germany & last for years. It weighs, it cooks, it chops, it dough's, it steams & stirs! We use it to make creamy soups & it makes the best risotto ever. This machine does the job of at least 15 kitchen gadgets you might have lying around the kitchen. A food processor & a blender will do all the jobs too. Some of you will have a vita mix, this too is a great machine, but more blender than food processor.

A DEHYDRATOR: If you are interested in raw food "cooking" a dehydrator is also a good investment. We can recommend the "Excalibur". Not only can you cook at 40 °c/105°F you can make your own sundried tomatoes & dry herbs from your garden. These come in 4, 5 & 7 tray configurations. You can cut any fruit up & dehydrate it, & at 40 degree cooking you preserve ALL the nutrients & enzymes. You will find more info on dehydrating in the info section at the rear of this book.

JUICERS: Simply put there are two juicers I think are worth it, both can juice hard vegetables & fruit & also the dark leafy greens & wheatgrass. Centrifugal juicers, whilst they juice quickly do not crush the cells & release all the nutrients. The twin gear juicers take a very long time to clean & are the most expensive. I use the Champion, which now comes with a wheatgrass attachment. Also the Oscar 900, from Vital Mix, (this is a juicer for 1 person really, if you need to juice for a family the Champion is the best,) both come with "blank plates" which allow you to homogenise & puree.

IMPERIA PASTA MAKER is the best make out there, it's simple & robust!
A SPIRALIZER (ours is made by Lurch)
LACKERMAN GRATER & ZESTER
GIGANT MULTI-PEELER (German fabrication)
GARLIC PEELER (rubber tube version) amazingly simple invention!
PESTLE & MORTAR a heavy stone one is best.
KNIVES if you are thinking of investing an a decent knife or set of knives, we would highly recommend Kai Japanese knives, made from tempered damask steel.
ELETRIC COFFEE GRINDERS are great for milling small amounts of herbs & spices.

EQUIPMENT

Excalibur Dehydrator

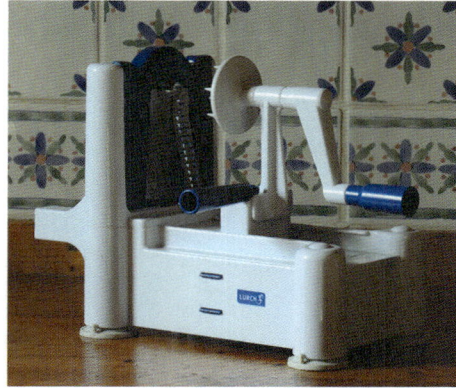

Spiralizer

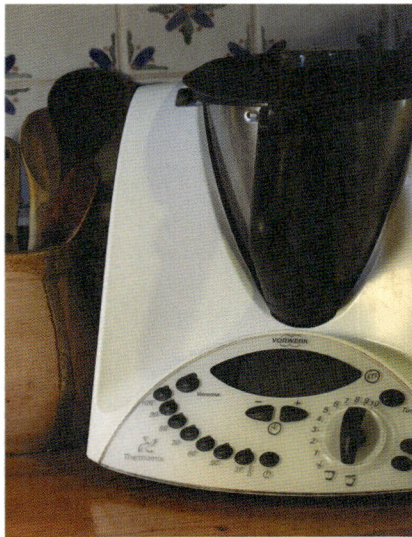

Thermomix

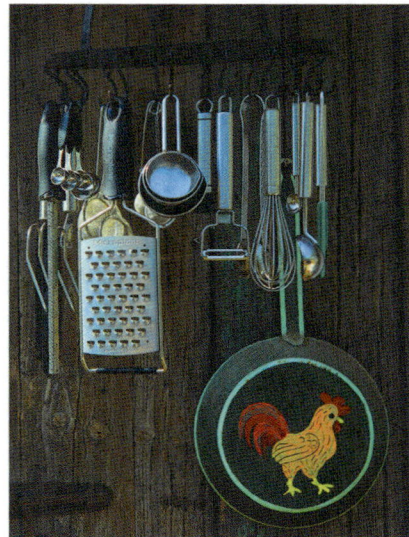

Every day utensils

PANTRY: ITEMS WE FREQUENTLY USE

Coco: raw chocolate nibs – coco powder 100% natural – coco butter

Coconut: cream & oil by dr. goerg.

Cream: Oatly www.oatly.com Provamel Cusine www.provamel.co.uk

Dehydrated: sun-dried tomatoes – porcini mushrooms – rice paper wraps – apricots – goji berries – dates – prunes – dried coconut - figs

Grains & flours: spelt (both brown wheat & white flour)

Herbs & Spices: a wide variety; see spices at the back of the book

Nutritional yeast flakes: a great replacement for cheese: they have all the B vitamins including B3 (Niacin) which has been used to reverse depression.

Nuts: cashews – walnuts – hazelnuts – almonds – macadamia – pine nuts

Seeds: sesame & black sesame – flax – sunflower – pumpkin

Oils: sesame – coconut – extra virgin olive oil – Argan

Paella: ingredientes & paella accesorios www.thepaellacompany.co.uk

Pulses: lentils – chickpeas – kidney beans

Salt: Himalayan salt - sea salt

Sauces & Pastes: soy sauce -tamari sauce (wheat free soy sauce) - ketchup manis is a thick, sweet, rich, syrupy Indonesian version of soy sauce containing sugar & spices. It's similar to soy sauce but sweeter - pomegranate molasses, the best we have found is "Al-Rabih" & "Anjar" - Tahini

Solidifying agents: Psyllium Husk – Agar-agar – flax meal – corn flour

Sugars: agave syrup – honey – date paste – date sugar – raw dark organic – stevia – xylitol

Vegetable Stock: our home-made stock

Make this veggie stock just once, & you will probably never buy supermarket stock cubes again It's amazing & it's without yeast! You can enhance just about any dish with your home-made stock. Or just place one teaspoon in a large cup & top-up with boiling water for an excellent cup-a-soup.

150 g celery
2 bay leaves
100 g carrots
a small handful each of parsley, basil, rosemary, sage or whatever takes your fancy!
100 g onion
50 g tomato
70 g courgette
1 clove of garlic
300 g sea salt
30 ml white wine
1 tablespoon of extra virgin olive oil

50 g parmesan cheese (omit if you are vegan or intolerant, it still tastes great) or replace with nutritional yeast flakes (very cheesy)

Roughly chop the veggies, tomatoes & herbs in a food processor, & process until everything is in tiny pieces.
In a pan add the salt, the wine & the oil & cook the processed ingredients for 20 minutes, stir frequently, after 15 minutes add the cheese.
Homogenize until it resembles a paste.

Stored in an airtight container in the fridge the stock will last 6 months, or place in ice cube trays, freeze & store in a container in the freezer.

Use: One tablespoon for every litre of whatever you are cooking works very well.
To have the bouillon effect (a powder) dry some stock at a low heat until the water is gone Then you can also use in dry seasonings

Liquid Lunch

Green Melon, Avocado & Mint Gazpacho, Rich's Gazpacho Pineapple, Aloe Vera & Lemon Balm Gazpacho Water Melon, Ginger & Mint Gazpacho Beetroot Gazpacho Ajo Blanco Hot & Tangy Tomato Creamy Cauliflower & Almond Spicy Squash & Coconut

Green Melon, Avocado & Mint Gazpacho   R
photo opposite

½ of a melon cut into chunks
2 cloves of garlic
2 cucumbers cut into chunks
1 ripe avocado peeled, & quartered
6-7 sprigs of fresh spearmint, (hierba buena)
6-7 sprigs of lemon balm (Melisa)
20ml apple cider vinegar
1 thin slice of fresh ginger
1½ tsp salt
freshly ground black pepper, to taste
olive oil add 20ml to emulsify & give gazpacho a glossy sheen.

Place all the ingredients (except the olive oil) in a blender.
Blend at high speed for 2 to 3 minutes.
Add olive oil to emulsify, adjust seasoning to taste & chill.
Sprinkle with mint, flowers or seeds & serve.

Rich's Gazpacho   R

1 kg of ripe tomatoes roughly chopped
1 avocado
1 red pepper
2 garlic cloves
30 ml apple cider vinegar
salt to taste
a good handful of either cherries stoned or strawberries
100 ml olive oil

Place all the ingredients (except the olive oil) in
a blender. Blend at high speed for 2 – 3 minutes.
Add olive oil & blend for another 10 seconds to emulsify
The Thermomix will blitz everything, seeds & skin, with a normal blender you might want to
sieve it to make it creamy & without bits!

R   <u>Water Melon, Ginger & Mint Gazpacho</u>

¼ watermelon chopped
1 avocado
¼ thumb of ginger
1 cucumber roughly chopped
1 garlic clove
6 mint leaves (spearmint)
50 ml apple cider vinegar
2 small tomatoes chopped roughly
salt & pepper to taste
a splash of olive oil

Place all the ingredients (apart from the olive oil) in a food processor or blender & blend for up to 3 minutes.
Add olive oil & blend for another 10 seconds to emulsify for a creamy refreshing gazpacho.

Pineapple, Aloe Vera & Lemon Balm Gazpacho   R

1 large ripe pineapple peeled, cored &
chopped
500 ml of fresh pineapple juice
1 large cucumber peeled & chopped
1 aloe vera leaf 10 to 20 cm long; cut &
drain for 5 minutes then remove spikes & skin
2 jalapeños seeded
1 avocado peeled & stoned

1 juice of lemon
1-2 tsp sea salt - to taste
1 small onion chopped
2 Tbs olive oil
a handful of spearmint (hierba buena)
optional to decorate
a handful of fresh cilantro, a few sprigs of
lemon balm (melissa) or pineapple sage

Place all the ingredients in a food processor (reserving a few herbs for decoration,) & whiz
at high speed for 2 to 3 minutes! Adjust seasoning & chill in the refrigerator.
Chop remaining herbs, sprinkle on top & serve.

Ajo Blanco "white garlic"   R

200 g raw almonds
2 cloves of garlic
1 teaspoon of salt
1 ripe avocado
70 ml of extra virgin olive oil
30 ml of apple cider vinegar
1 litre of fresh water
Finely chopped grapes & almonds for garnish

Soak Almonds overnight, then simply throw everything into a blender & blend until desired
consistency. Sprinkle grapes & almonds on top to decorate & add texture.
Sometimes the almond fibre makes the soup a little grainy, some people like this, & others
don't. If you don't then first blend the soaked nuts in the water & then sieve through a muslin
cloth (milk nut bag) or a clean tea towel, then blend with the rest of the ingredients.

R   <u>Beetroot Gazpacho</u>

To make this 100% raw, juice the beetroot & add 1 avocado to make it creamy.
It actually works better with cooked beetroots.

250 g cooked beetroot
500 g tomatoes
1 cucumber
30 ml apple cider vinegar
250 ml water
40 ml olive oil
salt to taste

Place all the ingredients (except the olive oil) in a blender. Blend at high speed for 2 to 3 minutes. Add olive oil to emulsify. Adjust seasoning to taste. Chill & serve.

Hot & Tangy Tomato Soup   V

1 kg very ripe tomatoes roughly chopped
1 Tbs apple cider vinegar
2 tsp brown sugar
1 tsp salt
a good handful of fresh basil

Reserving a few basil leaves for the garnish; place the rest of the ingredients in a heavy bottomed pan, over medium heat, let it simmer for around 20 minutes, stirring occasionally.
Once the soup has reduced, place in a blender & whiz until smooth & pips are no longer visible. Decorate with basil leaves, & add cream if desired & serve.

Creamy Cauliflower & Almond soup   V

100 g almonds
50 ml water
1 large onion peeled & chopped
a splash of olive oil
1000 ml of stock (1 Tbs of our stock for 1 litre is what I usually use) feel free to add more or less
ground nutmeg to taste
salt /pepper/cayenne
a few saffron threads (optional)
500 g cauliflower cut into small chunks

Put the saffron threads in the water & let infuse
Grind almonds to a fine meal in a coffee mill or food processor
Place the onions in a pan & steam fry (a mix of water & oil) until soft.
Add cauliflower, stock, nutmeg, salt, pepper, bring to the boil & simmer for 15 minutes
Add almonds & saffron water & cook for a further 10 minutes….
Blend & enjoy!

V   Spicy Squash & Coconut Soup

2 Tbs olive oil, butter or coconut oil
1 red onion, chopped
2 cloves garlic, chopped
1 tsp ground cumin
1 tsp ground coriander
1/2 tsp hot chilli powder
1 cm fresh ginger chopped
¼ tsp ground nutmeg
¼ tsp ground cinnamon
1 Tbs soy/tamari
¼ tsp ground black pepper
1 medium-large squash

500 ml cold water
2 tsp vegetable stock
1 Tbs lemon juice
1 tsp brown sugar
1 (400ml) tin coconut milk

Crunchy side dish
1 cup of pumpkin seeds
2 Tbs cold water
¼ tsp chilli powder
1 Tbs brown sugar

Add the oil, onion, garlic & spices & gently cook over a low heat for about 10 minutes. Keep stirring to stop it burning. Peel, seed & chop the butternut squash into small chunks. Add the water, stock cube & chopped squash to the pan. Bring to the boil & then simmer for about 10 minutes until squash is soft. Remove from the heat. Puree with a blender until smooth & then add the coconut milk. Return to the heat & warm gently. Add salt & pepper to taste.
Place the pumpkin seeds in a frying pan & toast lightly, add spices & toast them until they start to pop. Mix the sugar, chilli & water & pour into the pan. Stir the liquid, it will evaporate almost immediately. Remove from heat & leave to cool for a moment before serving in a small side bowl.

Salads

Sprouted Lentil Spicy Roast Aubergine & Tomato Gem Hearts with Fried Garlic Anti-oxidant Sprouted Quinoa Pad Thai Orange & Black Olive Roasted Courgette Pear Walnut & Feta Ensalada La Mota Shredded Carrots Alkalising Avocado Halves

3 cups sprouted lentils (see sprouting info)
1 red pepper seeded & cut into small chunks
1 avocado remove flesh & cut into small chunks
1 carrot grated
1 fresh beetroot cut into small chunks
1 cucumber cut into small chunks
a handful of cherry tomatoes cut into small chunks
a handful of physalis quartered (or other fruit)
½ cup sunflower seeds
½ cup pumpkin seeds
2cm piece ginger chopped finely or minced

Dressing
Juice of 1 lemon
2-3 tsp agave syrup
1 tsp whole grain Mustard

Mix the salad ingredients together in a bowl. Mix the dressing in a separate bowl.
Dress the salad, toss & serve.

V GF   Spicy Roast Aubergine & Tomato Salad (zaalouk)

It seems that every Moroccan Mamma has her own specific recipe. This is my favourite! You can serve this salad warm or chill & leave to marinate

3 large aubergines
500 g ripe tomatoes chopped
4 large garlic cloves chopped
juice of ½ a lemon or lime
a handful of fresh coriander leaves chopped
a handful of flat leaf parsley chopped

a generous pinch of sweet paprika
a generous pinch of cayenne
a generous pinch of salt
a pinch of ground cumin seeds
a pinch of freshly milled black pepper
a splash of argan or olive oil

Pre-heat oven to 240°C /475°F /gas 9
Wash the aubergines & pierce the skins with a sharp knife. Place them on a baking tray & roast for around 40-50 minutes. Meanwhile, place in a pan the tomatoes, garlic & salt & cook over a low heat for around 20 minutes, stirring from time to time, the tomato sauce will reduce & thicken.
When cooked, remove aubergines from oven & leave to cool, (if I am in a hurry, I hold the aubergines by the stalk & cut them open so that they cool quicker, leaving them to drain in a strainer). Alternatively, once the aubergines are cool enough to handle, slice open the aubergines & scoop out the flesh, discarding the skin. Place a strainer in the sink, & the aubergine pulp inside the strainer, & press the juices out. Then take an old knife & chop the aubergines inside the strainer, to release even more juice.
Once the tomato sauce has reduced (around 10-15 minutes) remove from the heat & mix together with the aubergine pulp, & remaining ingredients. In Morocco this salad is scoped up with fresh crusty bread.

Anti-oxidant Sprouted Quinoa Salad   R

photo page 30

100 g sprouted quinoa
2 handfuls of cherry tomatoes
1 broccoli head cut into tiny florets
1 cucumber peeled &, cut into little squares
2 cloves of garlic chopped finely or minced
1 small jalapeño chopped finely or minced
½ cup sunflower, pumpkin or any other seed or nut you like
a handful of basil chopped, parsley & mint

2 cups of red berries, such as;
blackcurrants, red currants
Raspberries, blueberries, physalis or any berry you can get your hands on.
Reserve 1 cup of berries to scatter on top of the salad
Combine the above ingredients in a large bowl.

Dressing
⅓ cup of olive oil
1 Tbs apple cider vinegar
1 lemon, zested

2 Tbs tamari /soy sauce
1 tsp salt
ground pepper to taste
2 tsp Dijon mustard

Place the dressing ingredients in a jam-jar, secure the lid & shake vigorously.
Pour the vinaigrette dressing over the salad, toss well, scatter the remaining berries on top & serve!
To sprout Quinoa - you simply put the grain in a jar & fill with water to about 0.5 centimetres over the level of the Quinoa & leave to soak for a couple of hours. Then tie a piece of mesh (mosquito mesh or muslin) to the neck of the jar & drain. Rinse every 6 hours & you will see sprouting activity within 24 hours.

Gem heart lettuce with fried garlic   RC

photo page 20

A dish from Andalucía, simple & tasty

gem heart lettuce cut in half
1 clove of garlic for each gem half
a pinch salt for each half
a splash of apple cider vinegar for each salad half

Simply chop the garlic into very small pieces, & fry in some oil (you want a light brown colour,) the garlic will keep frying when you take it off the heat.
Cut the gem lettuce in half, then cut a small wedge off the rounded underside, so they stand up in the dish without falling over.
Sprinkle some salt & vinegar on the gem heart & drizzle some of the hot oil & fried garlic on top of that.

V R   Pad Thai

1 cucumber peeled
2 carrots
¼ red cabbage
2cm piece of ginger (cut in tiny cubes)
1 red peppers
1 courgette

Sauce
30 ml tamari/soy
50 ml olive oil
20 ml sesame seed oil
1 Tbs tahini
2 Tbs agave syrup
a good handful of cashew nuts
zest & juice of 2 limes, or lemons
sesame seeds to decorate

Toasted sesame oil gives a special taste! However, use raw if you prefer.
The quantities depend on the size of the veg you have so basically copy the photo & if you have veg left over make some spring rolls!

Wash veg & slice in long thin strips, either with a vegetable peeler or a mandolin, careful as some slice really thick. Please see equipment page for recommended peeler.
To make the sauce whiz everything together with zapper!
Pile the veg, playing with the colours, red, white, orange, purple & green. Pour the sauce over the top & sprinkle black or golden sesame seeds on top.
Prepare to delight your taste buds & dive in!
If you can, get some fresh vine leaves or nasturtium leaves to give a nice green base to serve.

Orange & Black Olive Salad   V R

4 oranges
15 black olives
1 red onion, slice as thin as you can

Sauce
3 Tbs of olive oil

juice of one lemon
½ tsp ground cumin
½ tsp ground paprika or smoked paprika
a pinch of cayenne
a handful of chopped parsley
salt to taste

Slice the oranges into a half moon or rounds & arrange them in a pretty format, place the sliced onions in the same way. Dress with the sauce & sprinkle the parsley on top.

Roasted Courgette, Pear, Walnut & Feta Salad   V

This warm fruity, cheesy salad, complemented by the bitterness of the rocket & crunchy walnuts is perfect for summer & winter alike

1 courgette, sliced finely, lengthwise with
a peeler or mandolin
2 pears peeled & roughly cut into 3-4
cm pieces
200g feta cheese crumbled into large
chunks
100 g lambs lettuce
100 g rocket

1 cup walnuts
1-2 Tbs olive oil
1 Tbs Soy Sauce
1 lemon, remove zest & set aside
¼ cup fresh thyme (or lemon thyme)
1 tsp honey
salt & fresh black pepper to season

Heat the oven to 220°c / 425°f/ gas 7
Place 1/2 of the lemon juice, 1/2 of the thyme, a pinch of salt, olive oil, soy sauce & zest into an oven dish or shallow pan. Add courgette & pear, toss to coat in marinade & place in a hot oven for 10 minutes.
Meanwhile mix the dressing; the remaining amounts of lemon juice, thyme, olive oil, honey, plus a pinch of salt & pepper to taste.

Remove roasting tray from oven, toss veg again & crumble feta on top, & place back in the oven for another 5 minutes.
Whilst it's back in the oven, place the rocket & lambs on a serving dish. When ready scatter the roast vegetables, fruit & cheese on top of the lettuce, walnuts & drizzle with dressing & serve.

R GF   Shredded Carrots

5 large carrots shredded (or 1 carrot per person)
a handful of pumpkin seeds

Dressing
1 pot of natural yogurt, or soya if vegan
salt to taste
1 tsp ground cumin
juice I lemon

Mix carrots & pumpkin seeds in a bowl. Mix the dressing,
pour on top of the carrots, toss & serve!

Ensalada La Mota   R GF

I combine a mixture of the following ingredients, depending on what I have in the fridge, either grated or chopped up into tiny cubes, it's fresh & colourful.
red & yellow peppers – cucumber – tomatoes – avocado – carrots – raw beetroot - lettuce leaves – sundried tomatoes – pumpkin seeds – sunflower seeds – sesame seeds - walnuts – peanuts – dates – fresh fruit.

Method:
I mix everything together, with a honey & lemon, or pomegranate molasses dressing (bearing in mind the molasses is adding a cooked element). Or simply squeeze an orange over the salad, & add a pinch of salt & cayenne, an exquisite combination.
Toss a handful of fresh herbs such as; mint, basil, coriander, or edible petals.
Use whatever similar ingredients you have to hand.

R GF Alkalising Avocado Halves

These are especially nice for breakfast.
Also feel free to experiment with the ingredients you like, for example use pumpkin seeds instead of sunflower.

1 avocado cut in half
a small handful of chopped basil (you can use parsley &/or coriander too if you want)
a small handful of sunflower seeds
a pinch of cayenne powder
a handful of sprouted alfalfa (you should be able to buy this in the shop, or grow your own, see the back of this book on sprouting)
1 tomato cut in small chunks
juice of ½ a lemon or more if you like it tangy
salt & pepper to taste

What works really well, is a few drops of edible Argan oil if you can find it. It's quite expensive though, anywhere between 50-70 euros per litre. A lot of Moroccan people take a shot of it every morning for medicinal purposes; it is good for the respiratory system, for your skin & hair, along with other beneficial effects.

Take the avocado half & chop off the round underside of the skin, by literally a couple of millimetres, so that they sit without falling over on a plate.

With a sharp knife make vertical & horizontal incisions into the flesh (without cutting through the skin, as you need the skin intact). Then scoop out the flesh with a teaspoon so that it remains in chunks. Place in a bowl, & add the rest of the ingredients & mix together.
Fill the "avo boats" (empty skins) with the filling & garnish with some sprouted alfalfa.

Salad Dressings & Vinaigrettes

Some of these dressings are repeated in the book; & some are new! However, please feel free to "cross-dress" any sauce you wish, with any dish you want! Have a jam jar or a squeezy bottle to hand to make sure all the ingredients mix well. We could go on, & on with these dressings so we have chosen our favourites. Be creative!

V Yogurt & Cumin
1 pot of plain yogurt, soy yogurt, or almond cream
1 tsp ground cumin
juice of 1 lemon
salt to taste

V Yogurt, Lemon Balm & Mint
1 pot of plain yogurt, soy yogurt, or almond cream
fresh lemon balm & spearmint leaves chopped
juice of 1 lemon or lime
a teaspoon of raw agave syrup or preferred sweetener

V Spicy & Tangy Tomato
100 ml extra virgin olive oil
4 Tbs of tomato puree
1 Tbs ground cumin
juice of ½ a lemon or lime
Add all the ingredients into a cup or bowl & mix. Leave to stand & infuse for 5 minutes.

V Lemon & Honey, you can't beat it!
Juice of 1 lemon
1 Tbs honey or more if it's too sharp
Mix until you reach a balance between sweet & sour. For vegans replace honey with raw agave syrup, purred figs or dates. Feel free to add mustard, thyme leaves, fresh mint, cayenne, or whatever you fancy!

V Pomegranate Molasses
1 Tbs of pomegranate molasses
Mixed in, or drizzled over the salad of your choice.

Rubs - Dips — Sauces & Marinades

Alkalising Courgette Hummus Amalou Mahamara Jerk Pomegranate Molasses Duqqa Asian Marinade Fajita Mix Duqqa Roasted Curry Powder Roasted Pepper Cashew Broad Bean Dip Soft Vegan Cheese with Garlic & Herbs Plum Sauce Cajun Rub Fresh Green Chili Harissa Almond Butter Avocado & Peach Dip Tahini Paste Salsa Verde Garlic & Chive Dip Pesto alla Genovese

Being lime green in appearance, & its fresh taste of avocado, coriander & lemon, makes this dish a winner at the yoga retreat. We serve it together with our dehydrated flax crackers. Try & buy dried chickpeas & soak them for 24 hours, then cook in water until tender) otherwise use canned.

1 courgette with the skin on & chopped	pinch of cayenne
1 avocado	a handful of basil
400 g cooked chick peas	a handful of fresh coriander
1 clove of garlic	1 tsp Himalayan salt
juice 1-2 lemons	ground black pepper to taste
1 Tbs of olive, argan or oil	

Place all ingredients into a food processor & blend until smooth.

You can experiment with the ingredients; more cayenne, or a splash of sesame oil…

Excellent served with flax crackers! If you wish, decorate with sesame seeds & edible flowers.+

V   Amalou

Amalou is a delicacy from Morocco, it tastes divine! It's made from honey, argan oil, with crushed argan kernels, or ground almonds.

Traditionally, Amalou is eaten by the Berbers at breakfast or as a dip. It's an energy food, also given to children who are fasting during Ramadan

1½ cups almonds
½ cup argan oil - plus 1 tsp for frying
4 Tbs honey or raw agave for vegans
salt to taste

Firstly, gently heat one teaspoon of olive oil in a medium-sized pan.
When the oil is warm, add the almonds & toss until they brown.
Drain the almonds, making sure any excess liquid is removed, then mix them with the Argan oil & a little salt. Place in blender & whiz until they form a smooth paste.
Add the honey & blend for another few seconds. Pour into an airtight jar & refrigerate. The paste will last around 3 months if refrigerated. Amalou is regarded as a natural preventative medicine in Morocco.
For ultimate benefit take one teaspoon in the morning, & wait one hour before ingesting anything else, such as coffee, tea, etc.

V GF RC Muhammara
              photo page 40 (top right)

I thank my beautiful friend Chafika, for her extra special family recipe. Muhammara is one of the most exquisite Syrian infusions of flavours, ever!

250 g walnuts   2 Tbs pomegranate molasses
1 slice of bread or half an avocado   1 tsp Harissa (see recipe)
½ a small onion   1 tsp salt
1 red pepper   1 tsp cumin
1 heaped Tbs tahini

Chop the red pepper, onion, bread or avo into chunks & place all the ingredients into a food processor. Blend at high speed until you have a smooth, but grainy paste. If your paste is runny, it's normally because the pepper is too large; you can add a second slice of bread (or more avo) to achieve required consistency.

We also use Muhammara in our raw spring rolls. Enjoy!

Pomegranate Molasses   V

This isn't that hard to make, so have a go, it's worth it.

1 litre pomegranate juice (approx. 4 large pomegranates)
100 g cup sugar or maple syrup
25-30 g freshly squeezed lemon juice
We use fresh pomegranates, as they grown in abundance here in Andalucía.
Alternatively you can use a carton of organic juice.

In a large, uncovered saucepan, heat pomegranate juice, sugar,
& lemon juice on a low heat until the sugar has dissolved.
Adjust heat & simmer for around an hour, or until the juice
resembles a syrupy consistency, & has reduced to 1 to 1 ¼ cups.
(Don't cook it until it's too thick, as the molasses will thicken further as it cools down).
Pour out into a jar. Let cool.
Store chilled in the refrigerator for up to 3-4months.
If you like your molasses sweeter, add more sugar & taste, whilst cooking,
(allow to cool before placing in your mouth)!

Asian Marinade   R

Ideal for barbecues or marinate your tofu or Quorn!

½ a fresh pineapple
1cup tamari/soy sauce
20g ginger – finely chopped or grated
1 star anise
2 garlic cloves – peeled
½ fresh cayenne or chilli pepper (use powder if you like)
1 Tbs brown sugar

Mix the above ingredients in a small bowl, or place in a jar tighten lid & shake to mix.
Use as required.

V   Fajita Mix

1 Tbs corn-starch
2 tsp chili powder
1 tsp smoked salt
1 tsp smoked paprika
1 tsp brown sugar
¾ tsp homemade stock (dehydrated)
½ tsp onion powder
¼ tsp garlic powder
¼ tsp cayenne pepper
¼ tsp cumin

Grind the ingredients in a pestle & mortar, or whizz in a coffee grinder.
Use as needed in recipes calling for fajita seasoning.
Store in an airtight container in the fridge.

V   Duqqa
         photo page 40 (bottom right)

Duqqa is an Egyptian blend of toasted nuts, spices & herbs. You can use this spicy dry mix
as a seasoning, dip, or a crunchy topping for salads.

2 Tbs pumpkin seeds, hulled (husk off)   2 Tbs thyme or lemon thyme leaves
2 Tbs sunflower seeds   1 tsp coriander seed
2 Tbs almonds   1 tsp cumin seed
2 Tbs hazelnuts   2 tsp salt
1 tsp black peppercorns   Optional: mint or coriander leaves –
2 Tbs sesame seeds   chillies – 20 g grated parmesan – 1tsp
2 Tbs paprika   sugar – dried coconut

Place a small frying pan over med heat. Add the sesame seeds, cumin & coriander seeds,
paprika, thyme, along with any additional fresh herbs or chillies, & pan roast for few minutes.
Tossing the ingredients frequently so the spices don't burn! Warming the spices releases their
intense aroma!
Transfer to a pestle & mortar or spice grinder, & grind until the spices become a coarse
powder. Place spice in a bowl & set aside. Don't wash your grinder, you will need it again.
Add the pumpkin & sunflower seeds, almonds, hazelnuts & peppercorns & pan roast,
tossing the ingredients frequently, for around 5 minutes.
Transfer the seed & nut mix to your grinder, this time crush them slightly as you want some
crunchy bits.
Mix spices & nutty mix together in a bowl, & add salt. Sprinkle on all types of food to give it
a twist! Store Duqqa in an airtight container in the fridge.

Roasted curry powder   V GF

1 Tbs white rice
1 Tbs coriander seeds
1 Tbs desiccated coconut
1.5 Tbs cumin seeds
5cm cinnamon stick

1 tsp black pepper corns
1 tsp black mustard seeds
20 curry leaves.
1 tsp cloves

Once again, this will probably be too large for your coffee grinder so you might have to scale down the measurements.
Dry Roast the rice until brown, add the rest & roast until cumin starts to pop, then mill.

San Juan is celebrated in Spain in the month of June.

There is a mad exodus for the beach; cars are packed to bursting with tents, barbecues, firewood, inflatable rafts & huge amounts of food. In celebration of the sun's path peaking over The Tropic of Cancer during the summer solstice. The beaches all around Spain are covered with campfires, & at mid-night everyone strips off & rushes into the sea. As tradition dictates; dark spirits are swept away if you race into the sea at midnight, & wishes (written on paper) are cast into the flames of the campfire.
Richard had limited ingredients; however he still managed to conjure up & bring these two delightful dips, which we devoured in no time at all!

Roasted Pepper & Cashew Dip   V

2 cups whole raw cashews
1 cup chopped bell pepper
½ cup chopped celery
¼ cup lemon juice

1 teaspoon of Himalayan salt
2 garlic cloves
Pinch of cayenne if you want

Place everything in a food processor & process until desired texture. Dip away!

Broad Bean Dip   V

1 kg fresh broad beans in their pod
2 cloves of garlic
Some paprika (you can also use smoked if you like)

2 tsp of ground cumin
Salt & pepper to taste

Take the beans out of their pod & blanch for 2 minutes, & take the skins off by gently squeezing them out. Place everything in a food processor & process until desired texture.

V   Soft Vegan Cheese with Garlic & Herbs

This is so good, if you make it from a quality soy milk or tofu, it's difficult to tell it from a fresh dairy cheese.

1 litre unsweetened organic soya milk
½ a cup lemon juice (this is what you need for the tofu).

2 garlic cloves
1 tsp fresh thyme leaves chopped finely
1 tsp fresh chives chopped finely
¼ tsp salt

Place soya milk in a pan & heat, take pan off the heat just before it boils.
Add the lemon juice to the milk & stir briefly. You will see the soya milk curdle immediately. Wait 10 minutes.
Place a muslin cloth or nut bag inside a colander & pour milk into cloth. Wait another 10 minutes for it to cool down.
Then take the cloth by the corners & squeeze out as much moisture as possible.
You will be left with around 250 grams of soft tofu.

Add the garlic, herbs & salt to the tofu & either beat with a fork, or place in a food processor until you have a creamy consistency. Best eaten chilled.

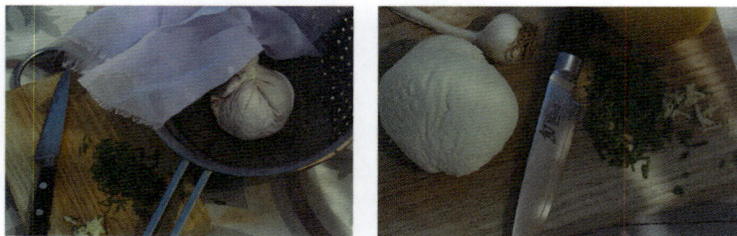

Plum Sauce V

You can use this rich tangy sauce as an alternative to ketchup or chutney. It also makes an amazing marinade for barbecues, or salad dressing.

2 kg ripe dark purple plums
1 large thumb of fresh ginger, finely chopped
4 large garlic cloves, sliced

1 kg dark organic sugar or whichever you prefer
1 litre apple cider vinegar or wine vinegar

Wear an apron or black clothes, as the plums will stain! Cut plums in half by slicing all the way around & twisting the plumb, this can be a messy affair so roll your sleeves up & get stuck in. Remove the stones & place the half plums in a large tall/deep saucepan.

Stir in the sugar & leave to dissolve while you chop the ginger & garlic cloves.

Add the garlic & ginger, & place the pan on a very low heat, until sugar is completely dissolved. You can test by pressing the end of a wooden spoon on the bottom of the pan; you will feel a crunching if the crystals are sitting there. You can also look on the back of the spoon to check that the crystals are no longer visible.

Once the sugar has dissolved completely, turn up the heat to reach the boil. Take care as the liquid will rise up quickly! Turn down to simmer & stir occasionally. Do not cover! The sauce will simmer away for 2 – 4 hours, enabling the vinegar to evaporate. Return to the pan every 10 minutes to stir. Once it starts to thicken you need to stir more often.

You are looking for a consistency where you can run the wooden spoon across the bottom of the pan, parting the sauce momentarily before it fills back in. Not as sticky as jam, as our sauce will thicken slightly once cooled.

When it is cold, zap it with a liquidizer to give a smooth purple sauce. If it's too thick add some boiling water to thin down to required consistency. Stored in sterilized jars this sauce will keep for 2 yrs, or longer.

Cajun Rub V
photo page 40 (bottom left)

This a fragrant dry rub, also for seasoning tofu, seitan, Quorn, etc.

8 cloves
1 tsp cumin seeds
1 tsp black peppercorns
1 tsp yellow mustard seeds
1 tsp of both paprika & cayenne

powder
1 tsp oregano
2 tsp dried thyme
1 tsp salt

Dry roast the seeds for a few minutes, then blend all the ingredients together.
Use this Cajun rub to coat your food. You can store in an airtight container for 3months.

R   Fresh Green Chili Harissa

Impress your friends with your home-made Harissa chili paste!

200 g fresh green chilies   2 Tbs ground paprika
100 ml olive oil   1 Tbs ground ginger
1 red pepper   1 Tbs apple cider vinegar
6 cloves of garlic   3 tsp salt
8 dates   zest of 1 lemon
1 ½ Tbs ground cumin

Place all the ingredients into a food processor & blend until smooth!
You can store in an airtight container for 6 months.

R V   Raw Almond butter

A fantastic substitute for dairy butter.

200 g almonds, with or without skins (however the skin does protect the almond from going rancid)
a small amount of olive, almond or argan oil
add salt to taste

Place the almonds in a food processor & grind at low speed until it resembles flour.
Add a tiny amount of olive oil at a time until you get a buttery consistency.
For a further creamy buttery texture, add a half an avocado!
Salt to taste, or add any other flavor you want to put in such as;
lemon juice or zest, garlic, herbs, spice, etc.
If you want a cooked version of this simply dry roast your nuts for 10 minutes & do as above

V Avocado & Peach Dip

2 avocados cut in two & scoop out the flesh
1 fresh ripe peach, peeled & cut into chunks
1 garlic clove peeled
1 Tbs olive oil
½ tsp salt
a pinch of salt

Place the ingredients into a food processor & zap at high speed until smooth!

V   Tahini Paste

We just love Tahini; we use this in our pad thai salad & muhammara pate. It also makes an excellent salad dressing mixed with apple cider vinegar.

150 g sesame seeds – toasted or raw whichever you prefer
2 Tbs sesame oil (toasted oil gives the tahini an intense nutty flavour, however use raw if you prefer)
2 generous pinches of salt
2 tsp lemon juice

Place sesame seeds in a food processor & whizz at high speed until you have a powdery consistency. Add the oil, salt & lemon juice, & whizz again into a paste.

Place in an air tight jar; pour on some sesame or olive oil to cover the surface preventing oxidization. Store in an airtight container the fridge.

V   Salsa Verde

This is a vibrant sauce; we serve it together with the griddled Mediterranean veg.

100 g parsley
2 tsp capers
170 ml olive oil
1 garlic clove
2 boiled eggs (omit if vegan)

50 g wholemeal breadcrumbs (use GF breadcrumbs if intolerant)
30 ml apple cider vinegar
salt to taste

Place the parsley, garlic, capers, vinegar, eggs & salt, in a food processor, & whizz until finely chopped. Add breadcrumbs & combine; add olive oil & process at medium speed until homogenised. Store in an airtight container the fridge.

V   Chive & Garlic Dip

150 g natural, soya yogurt or almond cream
3 garlic cloves – peeled
small handful of chopped chives
1 tsp lemon juice

Place the above ingredients in food processor & zap at high speed until smooth!

Pesto alla Genovese   V

You can make a million versions of pesto, however some recipes are simply classic, & this is one!

80 g basil
80 g parmesan (replace with 30g of nutritional yeast flakes & 7 sun dried tomatoes for vegans)
30 g pine nuts
1 garlic clove
½ salt
15 g olive oil

Place everything except the oil in a food processor & blend at high speed for 20 seconds

Add oil & emulsify for 20 seconds medium speed.

Pesto freezes well, alternatively store in a sterile jar & cover with 2-3cm of olive oil to prevent oxidation & tighten lid.

You can change the pine nuts for: sunflower seeds, almost any type of nuts, macadamia or walnuts are two of my favourites. Substitute the basil with: coriander, or a mix of both.

Sundried tomatoes need to be rehydrated by simmering them in boiling water (much better in white wine,) for 2 minutes to soften them up.

Jerk Seasoning   V

A taste of the Caribbean

1 onion, roughly chopped
1 chilli chopped
2 garlic cloves chopped
2 cm ginger grated
2 Tbs honey or raw agave or maple syrup
2 Tbs olive oil
3 Tbs tamari sauce

2 Tbs apple cider vinegar
2 tsp thyme
1 tsp all spice or colombo spice
1 tsp ground cloves
1 tsp cinnamon
ground black pepper

Blend everything in a food processor until smooth
Cut some tofu slices, then spread with jerk paste. For a more intense flavour leave to marinate for at least an hour, before baking/ grilling for 20 minutes.

Brunch - Snacks - Crackers & Bready Bites

Simple Bread Mix Living Muesli Cheesy Sun-Dried Tomato Scones Corn Fritters Spanking Good Pancakes & Ice Cream Spinach & Walnut Muffins Marinated Dehydrated Veggies Vegetable Crisps Dehydrated Raw Flax & Chia Crackers Garlic & Parmesan Flax Crackers Raw Pizza Base Raw Tortilla Wraps Nell's Naan Bread

V Simple bread mix
photo pages 54 & 55

You can replace the water with either beetroot or carrot juice to give a nice colour.
Be creative!

Heat oven to 200°c/400°f/ gas 6

340 ml of lukewarm water	1 tsp salt
30 ml olive oil	550 g of white flour or
25 g fresh yeast (or equivalent of dried)	500 g of wholemeal flour
1 tsp sugar	or a mix of both

Dissolve the yeast & sugar in luke warm water. If it's cold day, place the liquid in a warm place.
Not too hot, or you will kill the yeast. If it's cold, it may not activate.
Add the oil, flour, then the salt (be careful as salt deactivates the yeast so put it in last).
For less messiness, combine in a food processor & need for 3 minutes, or take out & knead
by hand, for 5 minutes. The texture of your dough will change from fairly sticky, to a silky
elastic like texture.

Dough should be sticky, get used to it, too dry & you will have a collection of crumbs which
will fall apart as you cut it, rather like mine, until Tracey got here!!!
Too wet & you will get it stuck on everything! Flour your work surface well. When you knead
your dough, it should droop around slightly when piled up. If you end up with a solid mass
add more water. Too wet add more flour.

Whilst you are kneading you can add seeds, olives or whatever you want.
Roll into a rectangle & place in the bread tin or on a baking tray. Leave in a warm, draft free
place, or cover with a plastic bag, leaving lots of space for it to rise (if it gets stuck on the
plastic, your bread will deflate). Leave to rise for an hour. (Try not to knock it when you take
the bag off so your dough does not collapse).

Then place carefully in the oven for 30 minutes, remembering not to slam the oven door.
If you want a crunchy crust then spray the sides of the oven with water as you put the
loaf in.

I use a 3 LB or 1.35 kilos heavy duty Traditional Farmhouse Loaf Tin, from Amazon. (This does
not stick! unlike others I have tried which have been as non-stick as super glue!

For proper bread have a look at: www.josloaves.co.uk
A great course on how to make professional bread & your own starter.

Experiment with: spelt wheat - beetroot bread – seed & nut bread - carrot bread
rosemary & sultanas – cheese breads – fruit breads – etc.

Cheesy Sun-dried Tomato Scones with Oregano & Pumpkin Seeds   V

20 g sun-dried tomatoes, re-hydrated & cut into small pieces
40 g pumpkin seeds
a generous pinch of oregano
1 tsp salt
½ tsp black pepper
½ tsp onion powder
300 g whole-wheat flour (preferably spelt flour)
2 tsp baking powder
2 generous pinches of cayenne
55 g butter
150 g mature cheddar or parmesan cheese grated
1 egg
⅔ cup soy or cow's milk

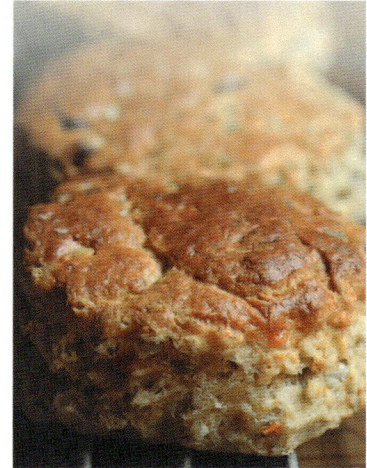

Place all the ingredients, except the milk & eggs into a bowl or food processor & blend well.

Beat the eggs in a jug & add the milk.

Pour the liquid onto the dry ingredients & mix until you have a doughy consistency.

Flour work-surface & with a rolling pin, roll out a thick dough; it must be at least 3-4 cm thick! Otherwise you will end up with flat cookies!

Cut to required size with a pastry cutter; place a sheet of baking paper on an oven-proof tray & bake at 200°c/400°f/gas 6 for around 15 minutes.

You can serve these hot; my favourite is with buffalo mozzarella & pesto filling!

Or they are just as good cold. However, if you plan to store them for a few days, place them in the freezer, as they dry out fairly quickly! Just remove from freezer 10 minutes before serving, or toasting.

R   <u>Living Muesli</u>

20 g oat groats   10 g sunflower seeds
20 g spelt grain   10 g pumpkin seeds
20 g barley grain
20 g quinoa   to serve: almond or soya milk
20 g rye

You can also add Kamut, Wheat grains & buckwheat if you want.

Soak everything for 24 hours in water, this will activate the enzymes & rid the grain of the enzyme inhibitor, which is not beneficial for the body.
All grains contain phytic acid in the outer layer of the bran, which if not treated by soaking binds with various elements (Magnesium, copper, calcium, iron & zinc) impeding their absorption.
Soaking allows the enzymes to activate & breakdown the phytic acid.
However if heated above 40°c/105°f this will kill the enzymes!
Rinse well before serving.
Buckwheat needs only 60 minutes soaking time, & on its own can be whizzed up in a blender to make a raw porridge. Buckwheat is gluten free & has nothing to do with wheat.

Topping:
Goji, dried apricot, dates, & dried figs soaked in either water or fruit juice for 1 hour
Use anything you want here, cranberries, raspberries, bananas, you choose!

Some people say that the grains are a little hard so here is an alternative way of preparing them:
Put the kettle on & boil 1 litre of water & wait for 30/ 40 minutes, then you will have 60 degree water. Although you will kill some enzymes & vitamins, you won´t kill them all!
Place the grains & water inside a wide neck thermos flask & leave for 12 hours, this will cook the grains a little & leave them softer.

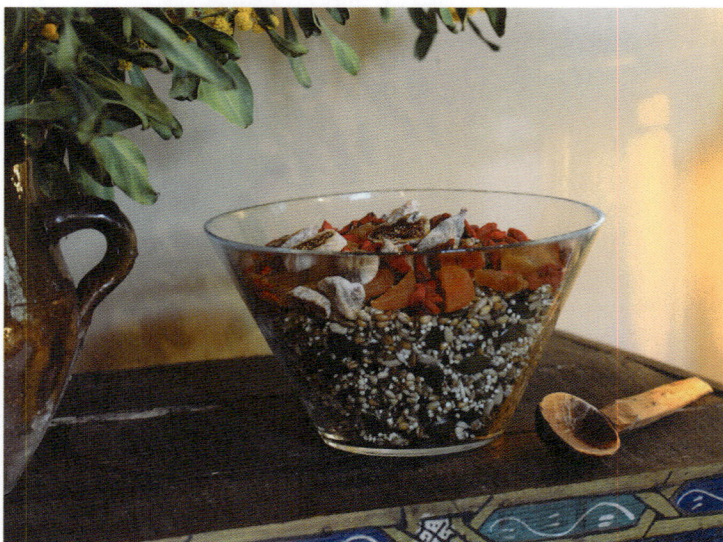

Corn Fritters   V GF
photo page 61

2 cups sweet corn
½ cup corn flour
½ cup corn meal
250 to 750 ml of water
black sesame seeds or poppy seeds

½ cup of chives (parsley or cilantro)
½ cup basil
1 tsp black pepper
1 tsp Himalayan salt
a drop of oil

Place all the ingredients in a bowl & mix thoroughly. Corn meal gets very thick & sticky, so you may have to add more water; you need a runny paste which holds together when spooned in the pan.

In a non-stick pan heat up a drop (literally) of oil, this means you will have a "dry" cooked fritter instead of an oily one.
Scoop ¼ cup of mix into the pan & spread out to about 7-8 cms.
This will stick to the pan but it is easily unstuck using a Teflon spatula.
Turn & cook the other side. Usually it should take around 2 minutes each side or until golden brown. The thinner you spread the mix the better. (Try avoiding using metal on Teflon pans, as it the coating is toxic if ingested).

Spanking good Coconut Pancakes & Ice Cream   V GF

Corn is gluten free

1 cup corn meal (yellow corn meal)
½ cup of corn flour
1.5 tsp baking powder
a pinch of cinnamon
a pinch of salt
400g can of coconut milk
1 Tbs agave or maple syrup

¾ cup water
a little oil for frying

Vegan Ice Cream
300 g frozen sliced banana
100 g frozen cherries, strawberries, or any other berries.

For the ice cream simply process some frozen cherries Stones removed) & bananas in a food processor (the bananas are what makes everything creamy) Of course you can freeze any fruit, mangos, kiwis, etc.

Whisk all the dry ingredients together in a bowl
In another bowl whisk all the wet ingredients
Add the two together whisking well to remove any lumps.
In a hot pan add 3-4 tablespoons of oil & then ¼ cup of mix (the mix should be runny enough to form a small thick pancake), cover & cook until the top just becomes firm & the bottom is golden, then flip them over & cook the other side.

V   Spinach & Walnut Muffins
         photo opposite

25 g coconut butter / or olive oil
200 ml of soya milk / almond milk
100 g spinach fresh or frozen
250 g wholemeal flour; you can use half corn meal & half corn flour if you are gluten intolerant
2 tsp baking powder
pinch of cayenne pepper
100 g of parmesan or 11/2 cups of nutritional yeast for vegans
1 egg lightly beaten, omit if you are vegan
200 g feta cheese, for vegans you can substitute feta with sun dried tomatoes or our vegan soft cheese works really well!
100 g chopped walnuts
sundried tomatoes optional

Preheat oven to 190°c/375°f/gas 5
Place milk & oil/butter in a large pan on medium heat & wait for butter to melt (don't bother if you are using olive oil,) then add spinach & then cool for 5 minutes.
Then add the egg to the spinach mix & stir in well.

Add all the dry ingredients, the flour & the baking soda into a large bowl, add the cayenne & freshly ground black pepper, then stir in parmesan or brewer's yeast & walnuts. Then add the spinach mixture into the dry ingredients & mix well.

We use recycled paper muffin moulds. If you prefer, grease a muffin tin with some oil, be sure to grease properly with either coconut oil, or veggie vegetable "lard"

Spoon some mixture into the tin or muffin paper mould (about half way up) then add a level of feta or sun-dried tomato. Then spoon some more mix on top, then add some more crumbled feta, make sure you push the cheese into the dough so it stays there.
Bake for 20-25 minutes or until firm to the touch, then leave to cool & take the muffins out & put them on a wire rack to cool. Super good hot or cold.

Marinated Veggies using a Dehydrator

Take a selection of veg, such as;

red & yellow peppers– onions – mushrooms – tomatoes – courgette – aubergine – broccoli – etc

Or a mix of wild mushrooms!

Either slice them or cut them into cubes (or florets), place in a bowl, & add 2-3 tablespoons of tamari or soy sauce, cover & leave to marinate for an hour or two.

You can add any herbs or spices you wish to the marinade.

Try marinating the veg with lemon juice, honey, garlic, thyme & a pinch of salt!

Place on parchment & dehydrate for 1 – 2 hours at around 105°F/41°c

They should not be dry, but soft & pliable.

These veggies are perfect for scattering on raw pizza
You can liven up the pizza base with almond butter or tofu cream cheese.
Or try adding them to our spring rolls or tortilla wraps.

For healthy vegetable crisps; Use a vegetable peeler to thinly slice the "crisps" leave in the dehydrator, until crisp, add salt & sweet paprika to flavour & store in an airtight container

V GF   Dehydrated Raw Flax & Chia Crackers
photo opposite

Apart from lubricating your intestine linseeds are one of the few foods which have the correct ratio of Omega 6 to Omega 3 essential fatty acids.
The other is hemp seed. The optimal level would be 3-4 Omega 6's for every Omega 3.
Most vegetable oils are very high in Omega 6's & not Omega 3's, some say that the correct ratio is 1:1…

Chia seeds originate from South America; they are very high in anti-oxidant alkalising minerals.

450 g linseeds – Flax seeds
50 g chia seeds
½ onion
1 garlic clove
1 Tbs Tamari or soy sauce

1 Tbs ground paprika
5 tomatoes
some herbs or spices according to your taste!

Grind the linseed & chia seeds & set aside
Add the rest of the ingredients to your food processor & process until you have a paste
Add the ground flax & chia to the rest of the ingredients & mix well, you should be left with a thick paste. If it is too runny then wait 10 minutes as the flax will absorb the water & form a gel.
Spread thinly on dehydrator sheets, & dehydrate for 6 hours at 105°F/41°c.
Then take the sheets away (so it dries on both sides) & dehydrate for another 6 hours, or until desired crispiness.

V GF   Garlic & Parmesan Flax Crackers

1 cup flax seed meal
½ cup Parmesan cheese, grated or nutritional yeast
2 garlic cloves
½ tsp salt
125 ml or ½ cup water

See above for method.

V GF   Raw Pizza Base

Use the same recipe as for the flax crackers & add 2 Tbs of tomato concentrate & loads of oregano.
You can add many things to this base, such as carrot pulp (if you juice carrots that is,) or soaked buckwheat (soaked for one hour) reduce the flax by half & replace with buckwheat.
The best thing is you cannot burn anything when dehydrating!

Spread the paste thicker to give more texture, maybe 3-5 millimetres.
Dehydrate as per the flax crackers; this will be a little chewy so dehydrate more if you want a crunchier base.
Spread the base with cream tofu cheese or almond butter & adorn with you lovely marinated veggies, sprinkle with nutritional yeast flakes for cheesiness, & sprinkle with fresh herbs of your choice.

You can have fun experimenting with coloured wraps! Try using beetroot or spinach to make red or green wraps!

3 cups peeled beetroot, courgette or spinach	a pinch of cayenne
3 Tbs olive oil	1 tsp ground coriander
2 Tbs lemon juice	½ teaspoon salt
	½ cup flax meal

Place all the ingredients, except the flax meal, in a food processor & blend at high speed until smooth (if using beetroot pass the juice through a sieve to remove woody bits). Then add flax meal & blend again until smooth. If it's too thick then add a little water. If it's too runny wait 5 minutes for the mix to thicken before spreading.
Pour mixture onto dehydrator sheets & spread 2-3 spoonful's & shape tortilla disks.
Dehydrate for 8 hours at 40°c/105°f, or until you are able to peel of the sheet, you don't want to dry them out completely; they need to be dry to the touch, but still flexible enough to roll!
Try putting some of your marinated dehydrated veggies in, or the falafel, or both!

Nell´s Naan Bread   V

200 ml hand-hot milk or soy milk	
1 tsp sugar	2 Tbs olive oil
25 g fresh yeast	125 g natural yogurt or soy yogurt
450 g spelt whole-wheat flour	1 egg beaten
1 tsp baking powder	olive oil for frying

Place yeast & sugar into warm milk, stir & leave in a warm place for 10 minutes, or until frothy on top. Place milk into a bowl & add the flour, followed by all the remaining ingredients. Knead the dough for at least 10 minutes, until silky & elastic.

Or place in food processor with a dough hook for 3 minutes.

Cut or pull a piece of dough the size of a tennis ball & roll out on a floured surface, to resemble a Frisbee, or smaller depending on the size of your frying pan.
Pre-heat a frying pan over a medium heat, when pan is hot, add half a teaspoon of olive oil to pan, followed by the bread. It will start to form pockets of air within a minute. Flip the bread when brown, adding a splash of olive oil if pan is dry.

When you have had your fill, & there is dough left over, you can cut some ring donuts, leave them to rise on a well-floured surface, otherwise they will stick & deflate when handled. Once doubled in size, pick them up softly & swiftly place them in fresh hot oil & deep fry for 2 – 3 minutes each side. Drain on kitchen paper momentarily before you get stuck in, they´re great!

Something More Substantial

African Coconut Curry Tofu Rich & Decadent Lasagne Courgette
Lasagne Creamy Spinach & Mushroom Tart Steamed Wild Rice Falafel
Indian Curry Coconut Dhal Andalucían Chickpea Stew Britti Burgers
Roast Vegetables & Pineapple Creamy Tomato Pasta Sauce With
Spiralized Spaghetti Pizza Rich & Fruity Vegetable Tagine Couscous
Feta & Almonds Veggie Wild Mushroom Paella Mediterranean Stuffed
Aubergines Chilli Sin Carne Fajitas Spring Rolls

African Coconut Curry   V

I love this mild curry, the ginger & fruit juice work really well

1 onion finely sliced
½ butternut squash, peeled & cubed
3 garlic cloves sliced
8 cherry tomatoes
15 g fresh ginger finely chopped
1 Tbs mild curry powder
500 ml vegetable stock
1 Tbs lemon juice
1 tsp cayenne or harissa

1 cup pineapple juice (apple juice will do also)
100 g natural yogurt
300 g tofu, (see below) or you can substitute with the same amount of chickpeas, seitan, quorn, you choose!
¼ cup fresh coriander
salt & pepper to taste

Place the onion, garlic, ginger & squash in a pan with the coconut oil & sauté over a very low heat for 2 – 3 minutes. Add the curry powder & sauté a further 2 minutes.
Set the tofu aside & place on kitchen paper to drain, reserving the yogurt for later.
Then add the remaining ingredients into the pan, stir, cover & leave to cook over a low heat for around 40 minutes, stirring from time to time.
Cube the tofu & place in the pan, along with the yogurt stirring gently, heat for 5 – 10 minutes & serve.

Tofu   V
photo page 48

Fresh tofu in less than 30 minutes! Tofu is so quick & easy to make, forget what you have read previously & try this.

1 litre unsweetened organic soy milk
(Unfortunately, most soya beans are genetically modified)
50 ml lemon juice
You will require either; a piece of muslin cloth, nut/sprouting bag, or a clean tea towel.

Place soy milk in a pan & heat, take pan off the heat just before it boils.
Then add the lemon juice to the milk & stir briefly. You will see the soy milk curdle immediately.
Wait 10 minutes.
Place a muslin cloth or nut bag inside a colander & pour milk into cloth. Wait another 10 minutes for it to cool down.
Then take the cloth by the corners & squeeze out as much moisture as possible.
You will be left with around 250 grams of Tofu.
You can use the tofu straight away, or leave to cool & store in the fridge for up to 48 hrs.

V   Rich & Decadent Lasagne

Just because food is prepared without meat, doesn't mean it has to be healthy.
This is a rich heavy cheesy dish, if you make this with Quorn mince, most people don't realise they are eating a veggie lasagne.

For the tomato sauce
1 large onion
2 garlic cloves
500 g Quorn
500 g tin of tomatoes
2 tsp of tomato puree (concentrate)
2 teaspoons veggie stock

a glass of red wine
small handful of fresh oregano leaves or
½ tsp dried oregano
2 tsp extra virgin olive oil
salt & pepper to taste

(Option: replace Quorn with re-hydrated soy mince (follow instructions on packet.) Or replace with courgette, mushrooms, cauliflower, broccoli, carrots, or vegetables of your choice) Cut onto small pieces.

For the cheese sauce
750 ml milk
100 g butter
100 g flour
300 g strong cheese (cheddar, parmesan, or other)

Vegan creamy sauce
750 ml soy milk unsweetened or 250ml carton of Oatly cream & 500ml water mixed
2-3 heaped tsp of corn flour – mixed with a little of the soya milk.
1 tsp veggie stock
1 Tbs nutritional yeast flakes

Another option is that you can purchase a soy cheese product & layer throughout.

8 - 12 lasagne pasta sheets you can buy these or make your own. If using dry lasagne sheets, cook according to instructions on the packet.
200 g extra cheese or yeast flakes for the top

Let's start by chopping the onion & garlic finely, gently heat olive oil in saucepan. Sauté the onions over low heat, cook until transparent, stirring occasionally.
Add Quorn (or soya mince or diced vegetables) & continue cooking over low heat for a few minutes. Chop tomatoes if whole, (removing eyes from tomatoes). Add to Quorn mix, along with vegetable stock, tomato puree, black pepper & oregano. If you are adding a small glass of red wine, then add half of the remaining tomato juice. If not add all of the juice. Stir, cover & cook over medium heat to reduce sauce slowly. Tasting in 10 minutes or so when flavours have blended, adding salt, or soy sauce if required. It should take around 20 – 30 minutes, to reduce.

Meanwhile, grate the cheese, (setting some aside for the top) & melt butter in saucepan, on low heat. Stir in flour & cook for 1 min stirring every 5 - 10 seconds. Don't let it burn! Add a small amount of the milk to the sauce & stir immediately, stirring continuously until the roux (mixture) has even consistency. Our aim is to disperse any lumps that may form. Continue adding small amounts of milk until you reach thin creamy consistency. Once the sauce has stopped thickening, add cheese & black pepper, & stir until cheese has melted. Take off of the heat. Cover & set aside.

Excellent you deserve a glass of wine! Remember to remove the tomato sauce from the heat! Grease an oven proof dish that is deep enough to place layers inside.

First add a layer of tomato sauce to cover the base of dish, & then cover with a layer of pasta sheets. Pour cheese sauce over the pasta, ensuring to reach the corners. Place pasta sheets on top, & cover pasta in tomato sauce this time. Add, another layer of pasta, & cover with remainder of the cheese sauce. Sprinkle extra grated cheese over the top evenly. Pre-heat your oven to around 200-220, bake for 20 – 25 minutes.

V   Courgette Lasagne

Courgettes: slice length ways (0.5 cms thick) enough to cover 3 layers, make sure you fry extra as they shrink.
50 g semolina flour
2 packs of mozzarella cheese (in ball form)
fresh basil
For the sauce:
125 g of textured soya mince
2 Tbs tamari or soy

1800 g cans of chopped tomatoes
1 bay leaf
cayenne pepper
1 tsp homemade stock cube
2 cloves of garlic
2 carrots
a stick of celery
50 ml white wine

First rehydrate the soya by emptying it in a bowl & covering with water to the level of the soya, then add 3 tablespoons of soy sauce.

Finely chop the onions, garlic, celery & carrots & steam fry in some oil (steam frying is done by adding equal amounts of oil & water at the same time to the pan, this does not allow the oil to heat up enough to cause trans-fatty acids). When the onions are translucent add the wine then the soya, stir well & combine & then add the tomatoes, the stock "cube" & a pinch of cayenne.

The trick of a good pasta sauce is to let it cook, stirring frequently until there is hardly any liquid left. Tinned tomatoes are raw & so they need to be cooked well when reduced, set aside for later.

For the "pasta"

For the healthy version cut the courgettes to fit the dish as above except they need to be thin so they don't stay raw. You will need 4/5 levels otherwise it will look like you have a dish of sauce.

Then lay a level of courgettes, followed by a level of sauce & basil & repeat 4/5 times if you can.

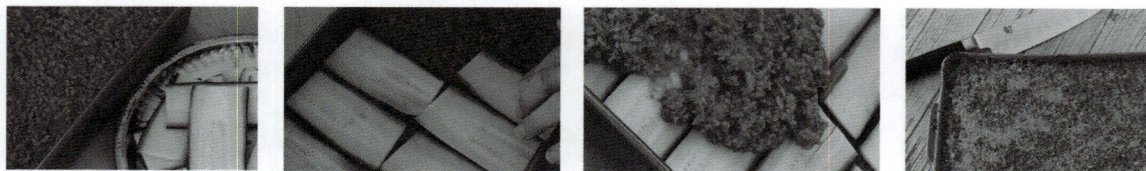

If you want to adorn the top with slices of cherry tomatoes then do as there is no cheese in this version. Or you could use nutritional yeast flakes to give a cheesy flavour

For the not-so-healthy version coat each courgette slice in semolina flour & fry until the semolina goes brown, & put them on kitchen paper to absorb the oil.

You need an 8x13 inch baking dish, this it how it is made:

A level of courgettes, a level of sauce, one ball of mozzarella (crumbled) & loads of basil, repeat 2 more times & then a nice layer of parmesan on the top.

Bake for 25 - 30 minutes on 200°c/ 400°f/ gas 6, & enjoy!

Creamy Spinach & Mushroom Tart   V GF

Pastry

250 g corn flour
50 g flax meal
90 ml olive oil
240 ml water

½ tsp salt
½ tsp baking powder
optional
2 tsp nutritional yeast flakes

Filling

1 onion medium sized
2 cloves of garlic
1 cup porcini mushrooms, or use feta (1 cup crumbled) & pine nuts instead (1/4 cup)
300g fresh spinach leaves or frozen spinach
1 Tbs olive oil
2 Tbs corn flour

½cup soy milk
1 tsp tamari sauce
1 tsp homemade stock
2-3 tsp nutritional yeast flakes or a handful of crumbled feta.
a generous pinch of black pepper
a handful of sesame seeds

Heat oven to 190° c/ 375°f /gas 5

Pastry: Place all the ingredients in a food processor & blend until you have a soft ball of pastry dough. Line a 22cm shallow pie dish, place pastry dough in dish form the dough to fit the dish by pressing with your fingers & fists. Stab the base of the pastry with a fork, in several different areas (to prevent it from rising) & place in oven for 10 minutes to par-bake.

Reduce oven temperature to 180°c/ 350°f/ gas 4.

Filling: Sauté the onion & garlic in olive oil over a low heat for around 5 minutes, until the onions are transparent in appearance.

Add flour & continue to cook on a low heat for another 2 minutes stirring continuously! Add the soy milk a bit at a time, whilst continuing to stir. Then add the tamari, vegetable stock, yeast flakes, & pepper. Add extra tamari to taste.
Pour filling into pastry case spread evenly, sprinkle with sesame seeds & place back in the oven for a further 20 minutes.

Steamed Wild Rice   GF R
photo page 76

We take a mix of wholegrain (brown) rice, with a handful of black wild rice thrown in, the result is purple rice!

Steam the rice in a steamer for an hour. If you are not serving straight away, let the rice cool. When you are ready to serve, heat the rice in a wok with a splash of olive oil or tamari sauce.

V R GF   Falafel

These are the best Falafels ever! It took us a few attempts; however we are real happy with the result!

1 cup pumpkin seeds
2 tsp ground coriander
2 tsp cumin
2 cups of fresh porcini or shitake mushrooms
8 sun-dried tomato halves, re-hydrated in hot water for 30 minutes
3 Tbs fresh coriander
1 clove garlic
1 small onion
2 tsp oregano
pinch cayenne
pinch pepper
½ tsp salt
1 Tbs lemon juice

Process all ingredients in a food processor until thoroughly mixed.
Form into Falafels & dehydrate on a silicone sheet at 40°c/105°f for 6 – 8 hours.

Hummus
½ cup macadamia nuts
½ cup of cashew nuts
¼ cup water
3 Tbs lemon juice
3 tsp tahini
a pinch of cayenne
¼ tsp salt

Blend all ingredients in a blender until smooth.

Or you can wrap these in our Raw Tortillas page 55

1 tsp cumin seeds	1 clove of garlic
1 tsp caraway seeds	1 large mushroom
1 tsp coriander seeds	1 stick celery
50 g Parmesan grated or 10 g nutritional yeast flakes	80 g walnuts
	50 g ground almonds (almond meal/flour)
a thumbnail size piece of fresh ginger	
1 tsp onion powder	1 cup flax meal
1 tsp garlic powder	½ cup oats
½ tsp smoked paprika	½ cup sunflower seeds
1 heaped tsp tahini paste	1 tsp veggie stock
1 Tbs tomato concentrate (optional)	1 tsp harissa or cayenne
1 small carrot	½ tsp salt
1 shallot	½ tsp tamari/soy

Grind the cumin, caraway & coriander seeds, & set aside.

Place the veg: shallot, carrot, mushroom, celery, & garlic in a food processor, along with the walnuts, & whiz until finely chopped. Don't over process or you will end up with mush!

If you are using a food processor, change the cutting blade for a dough hook. Otherwise place in a bowl, & add the remaining ingredients; parmesan, tomato concentrate, tahini paste, flax meal, oats, sunflower seeds, veggie stock, harissa, salt & tamari or soy sauce, along with the ground spices you set aside earlier.

Mix or blend ingredients together well.

Leave for just 10 minutes, for the flax meal to solidify the mix.

Form whatever shape you require; I normally form small burgers from a golf ball size handful of the mix.

However if you are serving in a wrap, you may want to shape them into the form of a small sausages.

Place on baking paper on a baking tray or oven-proof dish & bake at 190°c/375°F/gas5 for 15-20 minutes.

Once baked, you can eat them right away, or save them in the fridge for up to a week & re-heat. They also freeze perfectly well, so you always have a tasty snack at hand. Just defrost & heat in the oven, grill, or you can dry fry or shallow fry in a pan or skillet for 10 minutes!

ॐ

Indian Menu Suggestion
Coconut Dhal – Indian Curry – Nell's Naan
Whole & wild rice & Cardamom Burffi

Indian Curry   V

Not too hot, this curry seems to work for everybody. Select the veg you prefer & you can always put extra chilli in if you want to blow your head off!

a thumb size piece of ginger grated
2 cloves garlic minced
40 ml of ghee, coconut oil or olive oil
2 tsp mustard seeds
2 tsp fenugreek seeds
1 tsp cayenne pepper
2 tsp ground cumin
2 tsp ground coriander
2 tsp ground turmeric
2 tsp garam masala

1 red onion roughly chopped
400 g potato cubed
400 g green peas
400 g cauliflower broken into florets
1 Tbs of homemade veggie stock
juice of 1 lemon
400 g can of chopped tomatoes
400 ml of coconut milk
20 curry leaves

Fry the mustard & fenugreek seeds in the oil for around 30 seconds
Add garlic, ginger & curry leaves fry for another 30 seconds
Add onions & ground spices fry for another 30 seconds
Add potatoes, peas & cauliflower & stir fry for a couple of minutes until all the spices have covered the vegetables.
Add the coconut milk, tomato & salt, cover & simmer until the potatoes fall the fork when prodded.
Take the lid off & reduce the sauce until you have a rich creamy texture.
Serve with rice & enjoy!

Coconut Dhal   V GF

1 carrot, grated
a handful of fresh coriander finely chopped
2 tsp cumin seeds ground in a pestle & mortar
(or 1 to 1.5 tsp ground cumin)
2 tsp mustard seeds ground in a pestle & mortar
(or 1 to 1.5 tsp mustard powder)
3 cloves garlic finely chopped or minced
2.5 cm piece of ginger finely grated
1 large onion peeled & chopped finely
30 ml olive oil (or coconut oil)

1 tsp garam masala
2 tsp turmeric
1 tsp mild chilli powder
400 ml water
400 ml coconut milk
230 g red lentils
350 g tomatoes cut in 2cms bits
Juice of 2 limes (or lemon)
1 tsp veggie stock

In a pan add the oil, carrots, coriander, the ground/milled cumin & mustard seeds, garlic, onion & ginger & sauté for 2 minutes, then add the garam, turmeric & chilli & sauté for another 2 minutes.

Add the water, coconut milk, lentils & tomatoes & simmer for around 20 minutes, the lentils will absorb the water & cook, add the lime/lemon juice & cook for another 5 minutes.
Leave the lid on when you cook, & the result should be hardly any water left, leaving a thick paste.

V GF   Andalucían Chickpea Stew

Another dish local to Andalucía, it's a good time to clear out the fridge & use any veggies lying around!

1 whole head of garlic (roasted until blackened over the gas flame or in the oven, this will add a smokiness, Once done pop the soft garlic from the charred skin. (500g chickpeas, we buy them dry & cook them in a pressure cooker, or you can use precooked chickpeas for this dish.
a handful of almonds

100 g fresh or frozen spinach
½ courgette finely chopped
1 small onion finely chopped
1 red pepper chopped
2 bay leaves
2 Tbs veggie stock
1 Tbs smoked paprika
½ tsp cayenne

Steam fry (in the pressure cooker) the onions courgette bay leaves, pepper & smoked paprika until the onion is translucent.
Fry the almonds & break them up in a pestle & mortar & add to the pan.
Add the spinach, chick peas, garlic & cover with water to about 2 cms above the level of the chick peas. Add stock & cayenne.
Put the lid on & turn the heat down to minimum when the vapour starts to come out of the pan…
Cook for 20 minutes.
For those of you who are using precooked chickpeas use a normal pan, & cook for 30 minutes.
This can be frozen & eaten later; the flavours actually develop further upon freezing.

V GF   Roast Vegetables & Pineapple

This dish is one of my favourite warm salads; it's really filling, looks stunning & is really tasty!

1 red pepper
1 yellow pepper
1 courgette
1 cucumber
12 cherry tomatoes

½ a pineapple cut into chunks
1 Tbs soy sauce
1 Tbs ground Cumin
small handful of fresh coriander

Pre-heat oven 220°c/425°F/gas 7
Cut the peppers, courgette & cucumber into bite size chunks of 3-4cm. Place on a ovenproof dish. Add tomatoes; pour over the soy sauce, & mix. Place in a hot oven for 15 - 20 min, (or stir-fry over high flame for 10 – 15 min) Keep an eye on the roast vegetables, you want then to just blacken around the edges!
Take the vegetables from the oven, mix in the pineapple, scatter the coriander on top & serve hot or cold.

Creamy Tomato Pasta Sauce with spiralized spaghetti   R V GF

This is a really beautiful dish to impress your guests with! The rich creamy sauce complements the light crunchy raw spaghetti! It's a refreshing change to regular pasta.

Raw Spaghetti
1 raw beetroot
1 courgette
1 sweet potato

Spiralize the beetroot, courgette & sweet potato, cover & set aside.

Sauce
6 tomatoes
1 avocado
3 carrots
2 sticks of celery
8 dates
1 onion
4 Tbs olive oil

4 Tbs soy sauce or tamari
2 tsp vinegar
4 Tbs fresh basil
2 garlic cloves
1 red chilli or a generous pinch of cayenne

Roughly chop tomatoes, avocado, carrots & celery.
Put everything in a food processor & blend to a thick sauce.
Serve with raw vegetable pasta!

V   Quick Thin Pizza

Bearing in mind I make my pizza dough in the Thermomix, which only takes six minutes from start to finish! I normally have my topping prepared, as once the pizza base has been rolled out; you don't want the base to rise at all. Nell's naan bread also makes an excellent light pizza base.

Base
360 ml luke-warm water
20 g fresh yeast
1 tsp brown sugar
550 – 600 g organic white flour (use

wholemeal if you prefer)
1 tsp salt
2 Tbs olive oil

Topping
a handful of cherry tomatoes or 2 medium tomatoes
a good pinch of salt or garlic salt
freshly ground black pepper

a pinch of freshly chopped or dried oregano or basil
1 Tbs tomato concentrate optional
fresh buffalo mozzarella &, grated

parmesan, (if vegan use non-dairy cheese, or nutritional yeast flakes, or a soya cheese).
fresh basil or fresh oregano leaves

Heat oven to 240°c/475°f/gas9
Remove all other solid oven trays, you can leave the oven racks.

Zap the pizza topping in a processor for a few seconds, or chop tomatoes & mix together with salt, pepper, herbs & puree if using & set aside.
Use the same processor jug to crumble cheese; you don't need to wash the jug first.
Or simple tear the mozzarella with your hands. Use a vegetable peeler to slice the parmesan.

Dissolve yeast & sugar in lukewarm water, & wait 5 minutes. Add flour, salt & olive oil. Mix to a dough & knead on a floured surface for 3-5 minutes, until elastic & silky. Alternatively mix dough in a food processor using a dough hook for 3 minutes.

Cut a ¼ of the dough & place on a well-floured surface & roll really thin, using your body weight! Lift gently over your arms & place on a lined oven tray.
Spread a thin layer of tomato over the base & top with fresh buffalo mozzarella, or preferred cheese such as parmesan, cheddar, goats cheese, etc. If you are looking to make a vegan pizza, top with nutritional yeast flakes, or a non-dairy cheese.
Bake near the bottom of the oven (to ensure a crispy base) for 10-12 minutes, or until the edges have darkened.
Scatter your preferred herbs on top & serve while hot!
My favourite topping are: Sliced cherry tomato, buffalo mozzarella, pesto & rocket.
As well as Rosemary, grapes & parmesan, yummy!

I either place the remaining dough in a small loaf tin & leave to rise, & bake at 180°c/350°f/gas 4 for 20 minutes. Or I divide the dough into three; roll it out & par-bake. Then you can freeze pizza bases & use at a later date.

Rich & Fruity Vegetable Tagine   V GF

photo page 86

This is so easy! The key here is the spices, we use a 35 spice blend called Ras Al Hanout, the most only have seven or eight. We also use an intense spice blend called Colombo.

You can cook this in a big pan & then serve in a tagine, or see below for traditional method. All veggies need to be cut into thick long strips, lengthways, (this aids in stacking up the dish when you serve it.)

2 cloves garlic	1 red pepper
1 large onion sliced	1 potato
3 large carrots	a handful of almonds
2 small turnips	2 large tomatoes cut into wedges
1 aubergine	you can add pumpkin, aubergine, etc.
2 large courgettes	1 ½ Tbs of Ras al Hanout
1 ½ Tbs of Colombo	1 large tsp of homemade stock
10-12 dried prunes or apricots	2 Tbs tamari
juice of 1 lemon	1 large Tbs of pomegranate molasses

In a large hot pan, add the oil, & all the veg, except the tomatoes, leave them aside for now. Then add the spices & almonds. Stirring well, coating the veg in the oil & spices, sauté for 5 minutes on a low heat.

Add the water, to just cover the level of the veg, & then add the prunes, tomatoes & remaining ingredients. Leave to simmer for 20-30 minutes. Prod the hardest vegetable with a knife, when it slips off then cooked.

The traditional way to cook a this meal is in a "Tagine" (shallow dish with a conical lid.) The natural terracotta tagines are for cooking in, & the glazed versions are only for serving & décor, as most of the glaze contains a high percentage of led! This is why you should only cook in a natural terracotta tagine. They are really versatile; you can place them on the bbq grill, a gas flame (with a diffuser placed under the tagine,) in the oven, or on a brazier filled with coals.

Start by making your veggie stock. I mix my veggies in half the spices & use the other half in the stock (adding the molasses & lemon juice to the stock also). Make around a litre, as you may need to top up the tagine, whilst cooking.
Stack your veg in the centre of the tagine (rather like a circular pyramid.)
Pour the stock over the top of your veg, so just below the rim of the tagine base.
Place the tagine on a low heat. Keeping the carbon toped up! Check after 20 minutes by stabbing a potato or carrot with a fork to see if it's done, if not cook longer. Add more stock if necessary. Saha!

V GF   Couscous, Feta & Almonds

A Moroccan favourite of ours.

500 g couscous (spelt couscous is
excellent & maize couscous is gluten free)
500 ml hot water to soak couscous
1 Tbs argan or olive oil
100 g roughly crushed almonds

1 tsp caraway seeds
1 Tbs ground cumin
a generous pinch of salt
freshly ground black pepper
200 g feta cheese optional

First pour the hot water, tamari & oil over the couscous & leave for maximum 10-20 minutes. By now, the couscous should have absorbed the liquid. Take a fork, or use your hands to fluff up the couscous (running the grains through your fingers if necessary to remove all lumps). Cut the feta into cubes, add to the couscous along with the crushed almonds & caraway seeds, season with salt & pepper & mix again. Place the couscous in a serving bowl.

If you are serving this in our Moroccan menu maybe leave out the caraway & the cumin so as not to have too many flavours going on, or replace them with sultanas or other chopped dried fruit.

Moroccan Menu Suggestion
Aubergine Dip – Roast Pineapple & Veg
Rich & Fruity Tagine – Couscous Feta & Almonds
Walnut & Orange Blossom Halva

V GF   Veggie wild mushroom Paella

Ok, so this dish sounds a lot more complicated than it actually is. I would strongly recommend you buy a 30-35 cm Paella dish. It has two handles on it so you can twist the dish as it cooks so the rice won't get stuck on the bottom. If not try your luck with a normal pan, make sure it's non-stick.

Nora are Spanish Peppers, they are traditionally grown in the South East of Spain throughout the region of Andalusia. They are known for their sweet, fruity taste, which adds an intense flavour & colour to paella. "Carmencita", are available in most food shops, & are one of Spain's most recognisable brands of dried Nora's. The Nora peppers are also milled to produce sweet paprika.

If you wish to add dried Nora peppers: cut 2 dry peppers in half, discard seeds & stalk, place in a cup or bowl & pour over boiling water to cover & leave for 10 minutes. Scrape of the soft red flesh away from the inside of the skin. Discard the outside dry layer of skin. Use the flesh & the water as part of your stock.

1 large onion, finely chopped
2 cloves of garlic
1 red pepper
200 g of wild mushrooms, I usually use shitake simply because they have a wonderful taste
450 g of vegetables of your choice, I use peas & broad beans, artichokes are good also
400 grams of rice, "Bomba" rice is the best, if you can find it. Or try risotto rice Carnaroli or Arborio.
800 grams of stock. To make this put the water in a pan & add 3 pinches of saffron & a teaspoon of homemade stock cube, then add a half teaspoon of turmeric & the same of cumin. Don't go mad with these other spices as it will overpower the taste of the saffron. Simmer the stock when you start the process of cooking the dish. I would prepare 1 litre as sometimes the rice can get a little dry, & you don't want to be left short!

So heat up some oil in the Paella pan & add the garlic, pepper & the onion. Cook until the onion is translucent.

Add the mushrooms & fry until brown, then add the broad beans & peas. After a few minutes add the rice & stir until the rice is nicely coated with the oil. This is the last time you will touch or stir anything! So place the ingredients in the Paella dish to how you want it to look when it is finished.

Add 800 ml of the hot stock & bring the paella to the boil, then turn down the heat & simmer.

Cover paella with a lid after it's been cooking for around 8 minutes, this directs the steam to the top, cooking the rice all the way through.

The trick here is to twist the pan using the 2 handles bringing the left hand down & the right hand up & back again, you will see the rice not move as you twist the pan, this avoids the rice sticking to the bottom. Take the lid off when doing this so you can see if the rice is starting to stick, if the rice doesn't move with the pan then you might have to gently use a wooden spatula to un-stick it.

A really nice way to adorn the dish is to place asparagus on the top when you start cooking, like the hands of a clock.

It will take around 15-20 minutes for the rice to cook through.

Take a grain from the top every so often & test it to check if it's done.

Decorate with lemon wedges in-between each piece asparagus.

Now all that is left to do is to show it off to your guests…

¡Buen provecho!

Mediterranean Stuffed Aubergines   V GF
photo page 68

4 medium sized aubergines
1 onion
2 cloves of garlic
a handful of parsley
2 tomatoes chopped into cubes
1 tsp of homemade stock
3 Tbs tamari - soy sauce

a small handful of thyme, sage & rosemary
240 g barley (steamed)
a handful of black olives
a pinch of cayenne pepper
2 tsp of smoked or normal paprika
cheese for topping (optional)

Cut the aubergines in half & scoop out the flesh, leaving a half a centimetre thickness on the inside of the skin (set the flesh aside.) Simmer the skins in boiling water & place ½ a lemon in the boiling water; this will help soften the skin.

Chop the aubergine flesh to small chunks. In a pan steam fry the onions, & garlic until translucent.

Next add the aubergine chunks, smoked paprika, tamari, along with the veg stock & pepper. Cook for a 2-3 minutes. Then add the remaining ingredients; tomatoes, stock, olives, herbs & barley, & cook for a few more minutes before removing from the heat.

Place the aubergine halves in a baking tray (cut side up) & generously fill the skins with the mix. Top with the cheese of your choice, we use mozzarella here at the retreat, or sprinkle some nutritional yeast flakes on the top. Place in the oven & bake at 180°c/350°f/gas4, for around 30 minutes, or until the cheese is golden brown.

V   Chili sin carne

1 onion
2 garlic cloves
1 Tbs smoked paprika
1 kg tin tomatoes or fresh plum tomatoes chopped
2 Tbs tomato purée
175 g dehydrated soya mince or Quorn mince
1 Tbs tamari/soy sauce

1 red pepper
2 Tbs olive oil
1 tsp veggie stock
300g kidney beans soaked or canned & washed
1 tsp dried chilli flakes, this part we leave up to you for the strength. You can use fresh chilli too.

Soak kidney beans overnight in plenty of water, replace water in the morning & rinse again before using!

First rehydrate the soya by emptying it in a bowl & covering with water to the level of the soya, then add 3 tablespoons of tamari.

Pour the oil into a large pan, sauté onions & garlic over a low heat until transparent. Add the smoked paprika, soya or Quorn mince, chilli cook for 2-3 minutes. Then add the remaining ingredients & mix well to combine flavours.

Turn up the heat, when it starts to bubble, then lower the heat, cover & simmer for an hour, remember to stir every ten minutes or so.

Serve with steamed rice, nachos, tacos or tortilla wraps!

V GF   Fajitas

I love fajitas; they are tasty, quick & healthy. You can fill them with your preferred veg & eat them on the go!

Take a selection of your favourite veg & slice, such as;
1 red pepper
1 yellow pepper
1 small onion
a handful of mushrooms (shitake are best)

1 small courgette
a splash of olive oil
1-2 Tbs of fajita mix

Slice veg into strips, around 2cm.
Heat oil in a frying pan, add the veg & fajita mix into the pan & mix well, by tossing the veg in the air.
Cook for 2 – 3 minutes, & serve in a Mexican tortilla wrap.

You can add whatever you like into your wrap. Guacamole (see below), avocado slices, cherry tomatoes, grated cheese, yogurt or our soft garlic cheese.

Far East meets Middle East

1 packet of dehydrated rice wraps
2 kiwi fruits peeled
1 red pepper cut into matchsticks
½ cucumber cut into matchsticks
½ courgette cut into matchsticks
100 g red cabbage sliced very thinly
2 cm fresh ginger cut into matchsticks
a handful of fresh spearmint, coriander & basil leaves chopped finely
alfalfa sprouts (or other sprouts)
a portion of Muhammara

Start by making the Muhammara. Then slice the veg & fruit into skinny sticks approx. 4 cm long.
Soak the rice wraps in hot water for 1 minute (follow directions on the packet).
Place your softened rice wrap on the work surface & make a small stack of the fruit & veg.
Spread a large blob of Muhammara on top of the veg, sprinkle on the herbs & start to roll as illustrated.

Sweet Tooth

Chocolate Mousse Choco Cranberry & Coconut Slab Cardamom Burffi Key Lime Pie Chocolate Cheesecake Orange & Almond Cake Choco Sunshine Cream Paste Carrot Date & Ginger Cake Walnut & Sesame Halva Fruits of the Forest Sorbet Lemon & Basil Sorbet Banana & Strawberry Ice Cream Crunchy Mango Pastries Vanilla Extract

Chocolate Mousse   V
photo page 102

Chocolate mousse doesn't always have to be naughty!!

Base
300 g nuts of your choice (ground)
2 Tbs raw agave or maple syrup 100 g coconut oil

Mousse
1 cup date paste
100 ml of almond milk
3 ripe avocados
1 tsp of vanilla extract

125 g dark cocoa powder
350 g agave syrup (this makes the filling syrupy) however we use 180g of xylitol
raw cacao nibs to sprinkle on top

For the date paste soak 500 g of pitted dates in 100 ml almond milk for a few hours then blend until smooth. To make the base, melt the coconut oil, add 1tablespoon of the sweetener of your choice & the ground nuts. Mix & put a teaspoon or two into each glass & compact to form the base. Place in the fridge to set.
First blend the almond milk with the cocoa powder, until you get a chocolate paste, you might need to add more milk, so don't be scared! If you overdo it just add some more cocoa powder. Then place the remaining ingredients; date paste, cocoa powder, almond milk, avocados, vanilla & syrup in a food processor & whizz until smooth.
Put everything in a piping bag (here is the fun part)
Remove glasses from the fridge. Place the nozzle on the base, & as you squeeze the mousse out on top of the base you made earlier lift the bag slowly & allow the glass to fill up.
Sprinkle some raw cacao nibs on top & serve chilled.
You can freeze the date paste & use it as an alternative medium to sugar!

Choco, Cranberry & Coconut Slab   V GF

Simply an amazing blend of flavours

1 cup hazelnuts
½ cup cashew nuts
1 cup dried cranberries
1 cup desiccated coconut
10-12 dried apricots

¼ cup raw cacao nibs
¼ cup of unsweetened cocoa powder
1 Tbs agave or maple syrup
a few drops of orange essence
½ cup desiccated coconut for rolling

Place cashews & hazelnuts in food processor & blend until it resembles crumbly breadcrumbs. Add the rest of the ingredients & blend until combined to give you have a doughy consistency, with some crunch remaining. You should be able to squeeze a handful of the mix into a ball in your hand & it should stick together, if it's still crumbly, add more dates or a squirt of raw agave or maple syrup. Line a shallow dish with baking paper & press ingredients into dish as firmly as possible.
You may find that placing another piece of baking paper on top & using a flat bottomed object to press & smooth the top.
Chill for a couple of hours. Turn out onto chopping board, cut into squares of 3-4cm. Dust with coconut flakes, or decorate with rose petals, or other edible flowers & serve.
Store in air tight container & store in the refrigerator for up to two weeks.

V GF RC   <u>Cardamom Burffi</u>
photo opposite

1 heaped cup desiccated coconut, plus extra for coating
55 g mascarpone cheese
⅓ cup raw dark sugar
½ tsp ground cardamom (½ tsp ground ginger optional)

Place the pine nuts in a food processor or pestle & mortar & grind until you have crumb size pieces.
Add the remaining ingredients & mix well.

Make small balls with the mix & place them on a plate of shredded coconut. Whirl them around until they are evenly coated.
Chill & serve.

V GF RC   <u>Naughty Cardamom Burffi</u>

We thought we'd put this one in as it's rather naughty.

200 g of desiccated coconut (plus 50 g to cover the balls)
400 ml of condensed milk
a hand full of pistachio nuts, or any other nut you fancy. Ground in a pestle & mortar, alternatively cover with a tea towel & bash a few times with a rolling pin
a generous pinch of ginger & cinnamon
a small pinch of cardamom

Combine all the ingredients in a glass bowl & then put over a saucepan of boiling water, just like for chocolate, you want the condensed milk to go a little runnier. By all means try & do this in a saucepan on a very low heat, but beware not to burn the mix (as I have done plenty of times).
Once the condensed milk is warm add the coconut, nuts & spices.
You want to cook the mixture on a very low heat for around 7-10 minutes, stirring continuously
Then set aside & leave to cool.
Once cool make into balls about the size of a walnut & cover with the coconut you set aside earlier. Put in the fridge then knock yourself out once cooled!

V GF RC   Key Lime Pie

Base
100 g Brazil nuts
100 g cashew nuts (or any other nuts
you wish to use)

100 g toasted hazelnuts
100 g coconut oil melted
2 Tbs raw agave syrup

Filling
3 ripe avocados
50 g coconut oil melted
zest of 2 limes

juice of 3 limes
180 g xylitol or preferred sweetener

Base; place the ingredients in a food processor & blend to form a crunchy paste. Then press the mix either into a lined sprung cake tin, or in individual small glasses. The base should be around 1 cm deep. Place in the fridge to chill for around an hour.

Topping; Place the ingredients for the filling in food processor & blend until smooth.

If using a cake tin, spread the filling on top of the base 3-4cm deep.
Alternatively to fill small glasses, place the filling in an icing sleeve, & hold the opening of the sleeve in the bottom of the glass, squeezing the sleeve to fill the glass.
Decorate with lime shavings. Chill & serve.

Chocolate Cheesecake   V RC

For those of you who are passionate about chocolate vegan or not, you will love this divine dessert!

Base
250 g nuts (cashew nuts, hazelnuts, almonds, macadamia, pumpkin seeds, sunflower seeds etc) milled & set aside
20 g desiccated coconut (optional)

4 Tbs agave/or maple syrup
80 g coconut oil
3 Tbs of milled raw cacao beans

Filling
4 avocados (660g) scoop out the flesh
180 g cocoa powder

420 g agave or maple syrup
150 g coconut oil (melted)

Optional undertones!
Chocolate & Orange: 2 Tbs orange juice & zest of 1 orange
Chocolate & Vanilla: 2 tsp vanilla extract
Mocha: 2 Tbs of espresso coffee

Place the base ingredients in a food processor & blend to form a crunchy paste.
Then press the base either into a lined sprung cake tin, or in individual small glasses.
The base should be around 1 cm deep. Place in the fridge to chill for around an hour.
Filling; Place the remaining ingredients in food processor & blend until smooth.
If you are adding cranberries or prunes, mix them in by hand at this stage.
If using a cake tin, spread the filling on top of the base 3-4cm deep.
Alternatively to fill small glasses, place the filling in an icing sleeve, & hold the opening of the sleeve in the bottom of the glass, squeezing the sleeve to fill the glass.
Indulge yourself!

V GF   Orange & Almond Cake

This is an amazingly easy versatile wheat-free cake!

2 large oranges
6 eggs
450 g ground almonds
250 g sugar
1 tsp baking powder

Heat oven to 180°c/350°f/gas4
Wash oranges, place them in a pan of water & boil them whole for an hour, cool & remove pips with a fork, place in a food processor & whizz to a pulp.
Beat eggs in large bowl; add the almonds, sugar, baking powder & lemon.
Mix thoroughly & pour into a 20cm lined spring base cake tin, & bake for around 40 minutes.
If it's still wet in the centre of the cake, bake a little longer. Cool in tin before turning out.

Replace oranges with:
Lemon; 2 lemons
Coffee; replace oranges with 50ml espresso coffee & 1 Tbs ground coffee
Chocolate; 200g dark (80%) chocolate melted.
Or 200g cocoa powder & juice of 2 oranges, or 100ml milk (soy milk)

V GF RC Choco Sunshine Cream Paste

A healthy option to Chocolate Spread for kids & adults alike! Also great with Ice cream

210 g raw sunflower seeds
60 g cocoa powder
100 g raw dark sugar
a little soya milk, almond milk, or fruit juice

Place the above ingredients in a food processor & blend for 30 seconds. Add a little of the liquid at a time until you have a thick, but spreadable paste.
Or place in a pestle & mortar and work until you have a grainy powder (or you can leave some larger pieces for a crunchier texture).
Add a little of the liquid at a time until you have a thick, but spreadable paste.

Try adding mint or orange zest for a variation in flavour.

Carrot, Date & Ginger Cake   V
photo page 96

This is a rich moist cake that is real easy to make. One of our favourites!

200 g brown sugar
200 ml mild olive oil
3 eggs (room temperature)
200 g whole wheat flour
100 g course semolina flour
2 tsp baking powder
1 tsp bicarbonate of soda
1 large thumb of fresh ginger, diced
1 Tbs poppy seeds

100 g medjool dates, stoned & sliced
into thick rounds
200 g carrots grated
1 apple coarsely grated
2 tsp ground cinnamon
2 tsp ground ginger
1 tsp grated or ground nutmeg
100 g walnuts optional

Pre-heat oven to 270 °C/325°F/gas mark 3
Place the eggs, sugar & oil in either a food processor, or alternatively in a large bowl & whisk thoroughly until smooth & well aerated.
Add all the dry ingredients into the bowl & mix well.
Then add the remaining ingredients, carrots, dates, ginger & apple.
If you are using a food processor, take care not to pulp the ginger & dates.
Place in a 20cm lined spring based cake tin & bake for an hour.
Alternatively, line a roasting pan, & bake for around 50 minutes. Depending if you want to serve slices or squares.

It's often recommended to remove from oven & leave to cool before slicing; however I can never wait that long, & its real good hot! Just cover the cut end when leaving to cool, so it doesn't dry out.
Serve with crème fresh, mascarpone cheese, or almond cream!

Walnut & Sesame Halva with Orange Blossom or Rose Water   R V GF
photo page 106

This is basically a delicious fragrant middle-eastern energy bar

250 g walnuts
250 g almonds
50 g sesame Seeds

400 g medjool dates (we sometimes
add a handful of goji berries also)
3 tsp orange blossom or rose water

Place all the ingredients in a food processor & blend until sticky, but some crunch still remains. You should be able to squeeze a handful of the mix into a ball in your hand & it should stick together, if it's still crumbly, add more dates or a squirt of raw agave or maple syrup.
Line a shallow dish with baking paper & press ingredients into dish as firmly as possible. You may find that placing another piece of baking paper on top & using a flat bottomed object to press & smooth the halva.
Chill for a couple of hours. Turn out onto chopping board, cut into squares of 3-4cm. Dust with icing sugar, decorate with rose petals, or other edible flowers & serve.

Fruits of the Forest Sorbet   R V
photo opposite

There is nothing more refreshing on a hot summer's day than a glass of sorbet. It's so quick & easy to make in the Thermomix, please check that your food processor is of the standard to crush ice cubes!

50 g sugar or maple syrup (depending on how ripe the fruit is you might have to add more sugar)
500 g frozen fruits (mango, pineapple, melon, passion fruit)
200 g ice cubes
Fragrant rose petals optional

Place sugar in a food processor & grind to make powdered sugar.

Clear sides of bowl with a spatula, & add remaining ingredients
Take the ice cubes out of the freezer for a few minutes before processing, this will ensure a smoother consistency. Wet the ice cubes first so they don't stick.
Put the ice & fruit in with the sugar

Mix for about 30 seconds, or until no ice chunks remain. Serve immediately as a soft sorbet in chilled glass or bowl, or re-freeze to further solidify if serving later.

Lemon & Basil Sorbet   R V GF

120 g sugar
50 g fresh basil
100 g frozen lemon (slices or pieces)
zest from 1 lemon
200-250 g ice cubes or frozen milk cubes (freeze in ice cube trays) you can use coconut milk, yogurt, soy milk, almond milk or cream.

Please see above for methodology

Banana & Strawberry Ice cream   R V GF

3 frozen bananas sliced
6 frozen strawberries
Place in food processor & blend for 1 minute, or until creamy

V Crunchy Mango Pastries

We make these mouth-watering pastries with a mango filling, however you can fill these small pies with any other fruit or savoury filling of your choice. Spinach is one of my favourites.

Pastry
250 g organic butter – use vegetable suet if vegan
500 g strong white flour, plus a little extra for dusting the work surface

a little cold water to bind

Filling
2 large mango's peeled & cut into fine cubes

Place the butter or veg suet in the freezer for at least 4 hours before you start! The secret here is in the pastry, you need to handle the pastry dough as little as possible (if at all)! Once you take the butter from the freezer work as swiftly as possible.

Preheat oven to 200°c /400°f/gas6

Place the flour in a large bowl, & take the butter from the freezer.
Place a little of the flour on the work surface, & placing the grater on top, grate the butter, being careful that your hand doesn't slip once greasy (it's painful). Once you have grated half the butter scoop it up with a flat instrument & toss it into the bowl & lift with a fork to coat the butter in flour. Grate the rest of the butter, add to bowl & lightly toss with a fork until evenly distributed.
Add a small amount of cold water to make stiff dough, mixing as little as possible.
Flour the work surface well! For best results: aim to cut as many rounds with the cutter from this first sheet, without rolling a second time; as over-rolling will dissipate the buttery particles, & you will lose the crispness. So keep your rolling action to the required minimum, to reach a thin layer of pastry.

Cut with 12 cm round pastry cutters, slip a pallet knife underneath & transfer to a lined baking sheet.
I leave half my circles hanging off the sides of the baking tray, as they will later be folded over as the pie lid. Place a heaped teaspoon of the chopped mangos on one half of the circle in a half-moon shape, adding a touch of spice, such as cinnamon or ginger if you wish.
Dampen the edges with milk (or soy milk) to make a good seal. Fold the empty half of the pastry disk over the filling & press to seal. Brush tops with milk & pierce two small slits in the top with a sharp knife to release pressure during baking.
Bake for 15 – 20 minutes. They should be a lovely golden colour. Best eaten hot, however they are also good cold for picnic or snacks.

R V GF Vanilla Extract

This is far better than anything you can buy in the store! Well worth the wait.

6 – 8   vanilla pods
1 cup   good quality brandy or vodka

Stand the vanilla pods vertically in a small jar, top up with alcohol (to cover pods) & tighten lid. Let the jar stand in a dark place for 6 – 8 weeks; turning the jar occasionally to aid the infusion process.

Infusions

Hot infusions: You may choose to make a hot infusion with boiling water. However, to benefit the most from an infusion it's best to either boil the kettle & leave for around 10 minutes until the water has cooled to around 70°c/160°f. You can drink these immediately or leave them to stand a while.

Cold – Raw infusions: place your desired herbs, flowers, etc. in a glass tea pot or a glass bottle. Top up with cold water & leave in a sunny window, or alternatively place in a sunny spot in the garden. This will reach around 40°c/105°f. Leave it to infuse for at least 4 hours, preferably 24 hours.
Once fully infused, you can store in the fridge for up to 4 days.

You can make such delicious infusions from almost anything. I have listed a few ingredients below, try combining them to create different blends & flavours!

Dehydrated fruits such as: apple – guava – mandarin – peach – physalis - berries

Dried: French marigold (tagetes patula) kills tummy fungus - rose petals – hibiscus flowers – jasmine

Fresh herbs: Louisa leaves- coriander – spearmint – sage – lemon thyme

Lemon – orange - ginger – ginseng - cinnamon – cardamom - star anise

Almond Milk & Cream

This is such a good alternative to milk; you will absorb more calcium from a glass of this alkalising milk than a glass of acidifying dairy milk.

220g almonds, you can also add other nuts & seeds too, brazil nuts (high in the antioxidant Selenium) & hemp seeds (high in essential fatty acids)
1 litre of water
Soak the almonds overnight

Rinse & blend everything, then pass through a nut bag to filter out the fibre (which you can use for cookies) or simply use a clean tea towel
Add some dates, before you blend, to sweeten. Even a pinch of cinnamon works well.
If you want it creamier, add more almonds!

Tbs/tablespoon
tsp/teaspoon

OUR Conversions?..

Cups? Grams? Ounces? Handfuls? Pinches? Kilos? Tonnes? Teaspoons? Levelled? or not?.....

A little confusing....
So here it is... an approximate table of ounces to grams.
Personally we prefer cups so we don't have to weigh everything constantly which means that we have some recipes with cups so buy yourself a set!

Weights

Imperial	Metric
½ oz	10 g
¾ oz	20 g
1 oz	25 g
1½ oz	40 g
2 oz	50 g
2½ oz	60 g
3 oz	75 g
4 oz	110 g
4½ oz	125 g
5 oz	150 g
6 oz	175 g
7 oz	200 g
8 oz	225 g
9 oz	250 g
10 oz	275 g
12 oz	350 g
1 lb	450 g
1 lb 8 oz	700 g
2 lb	900 g
3 lb	1.35 kg

Oven Temperatures

Gas	F	C
1	275 F	140 C
2	300 F	150 C
3	325 F	170 C
4	350 F	180 C
5	375 F	190 C
6	400 F	200 C
7	425 F	220 C
8	450 F	230 C
9	475 F	240 C

CENTRO PUNTO DE LUZ
YOGA RETREAT

EL CAÑUELO – PERIANA – ANDALUCIA

WWW.CENTROPUNTODELUZ.COM

PHOTOGRAPHY & DESIGN BY:

PAPAGOZ

NELL & NEPH ART

AURA ENERGY PHOTOGRAPHY:

EDWARD MURPHY

CONTACT: CRUDEFOOD@CENTROPUNTODELUZ.COM

ALL THE INFO YOU NEED TO MAKE HEALTHY CHANGES TO YOUR DIET

HOME REMEDIES

CAYENNE PEPPER

This is the only one I will talk about because if you could choose just one all-round remedy then THIS would be it. I won't sit here & regurgitate Conrad LeBeau's material (see resources page), just get his books; they are inexpensive & short & absolutely amazing! I will talk about some of my personal successful experiences with these inexpensive products.

1. Anti-Irritant Properties
2. Anti-Cold & Flu Agent breaks up mucus
3. Anti-Fungal Properties
4. Anti-Allergen
5. Digestive Aid, stimulates the digestive tract
6. Helps Produce Saliva
7. Useful for Blood Clots, this spice has been known to stop heart attacks in 1 minute! For maintenance drink hot water & cayenne every day/ or 1 capsule
8. Detox Support, combined with lemon juice & honey, cayenne tea is an excellent morning beverage.
9. Joint-Pain Reliever
10. Anti-Bacterial Properties
11. Supports Weight Loss. Cayenne is also a great metabolic-booster, aiding the body in burning excess amounts of fats.
12. Improves Heart-Health, cayenne helps to keep blood pressure levels normalized.
13. Remedy for Toothache
14. Topical Remedy, don't be scared, if you cut yourself put this on the cut, it burns less than when you eat it. Much of cayenne's healing action occurs right in your mouth. As cayenne touches your tongue, the cayenne absorbs in seconds & nerve endings send signals throughout the body - sending waves of fresh blood to wherever you are sick.

Healing begins in seconds! There are case studies where heart attacks have been stopped in seconds by hot water & cayenne! This is truly a wonderful spice, use it every day, it will be in most recipes in this book, you can find these case studies on www.herballegacy.com. Look up Ulcers whilst you're at it! You can also subscribe to a free newsletter.

Scientific studies performed by the Department of Haematology/Oncology at Cedars Sinai Medical Centre in Los Angeles, California have shown that consumption of habanero peppers can offer a beneficial effect against prostate cancer.

GOOD FATS, BAD FATS...

SIMPLY PUT, THE BODY NEEDS FATS, they are important. Also there is a reason why we hear "essential fatty acids" being mentioned all the time. Essential means we cannot produce these ourselves & so have to ingest them. The question is which ones?

SOME FATS SLOW YOU DOWN, others increase your energy. Some fats make you fat, others keep you slim. Some fats cause inflammation, others decrease it. Some fats relieve allergies others worsen them. Some fats clog your arteries, others clean your arteries" (Udo Erasmus, "Fats that heal fats that kill"). It's funny, we either seem to be having a low fat diet or a very high fat diet, or eating certain fats thinking they are healthy but in fact are not. There are several processes that turn good fats into bad:

HYDROGENATION which turns oils into cheap spreadable long life fats. There are less & less of these nowadays.

FRYING, which we all know is bad for us as it produces trans-fatty acids which can eventually clog your arteries. (When frying onions, for example, use equal amounts of water & oil to keep the temperature of the oil down to 100°c/215°f, this is a way of frying which is a little healthier).
If you must fry then coconut oil has the highest burn rate, (it can withstand higher temperatures) & is one of the safest. With sunflower being one of the worst, due to refining & the deodorising process, produces colourless, odourless, & tasteless oils.

EVEN WHEN WE EAT HEALTHY FATS; such as nuts, seeds, & other natural fats such as animal, we tend to eat far too many. Many of us are sat at a desk nowadays; we are no longer working outside burning lots of carbs with physical work like our grandparents. We have become sedentary, so we need far less fuel. Consume in moderation!

OMEGA 3 & 6, ESSENTIAL FATTY ACIDS.
Essential fatty acids:
- Increase energy production by helping the body obtain more oxygen
- Increase metabolic rate & energy levels so we burn more calories.
- Keep us slimmer, in the right dose.
- Increase brain development & function, the brain is 60 % fat.
- Promote heart health
- Protect our DNA from damage.
- Protect our skin, nails & hair by reducing dehydration.
- Are also required for the liver & digestive system.
- Also help maintain the flexibility of the cellular membranes.

GOOD FATS, BAD FATS, CONT...

GOOD SOURCES of vegan omega 3's & 6's are linseed & hemp seed.
Fats that come from nature are all good; it is the way we process & consume them that makes them bad....

A NUMBER OF FATS which are cold pressed, are good for you in moderation. Out of those there are some very delicate ones which should be kept in a dark bottle in the fridge, for example hemp seed oil & linseed oil. This is because they go rancid & oxidise easily & produce the free radicals! If we consume all fats in their natural state then they can be beneficial, it is when we start to fry, cook & process them that the problems start. But we are not going to stop cooking with fats altogether are we? So here is an idea of which fats are the best for cooking. All other fats should be cold pressed, this means you have to buy them in health food shops & are quite expensive. Then again you only need little quantities for salads for example. The exception is olive oil, as it is easily found in most countries.

OLIVE OIL; use equal parts of oil & water at the same time to fry your garlic & onions, this keeps the oil at 100°c/212°f& does not allow it to burn

COCONUT OIL; because the fatty acids are mainly saturated it makes it very resistant to oxidation at high levels of heat. This is one of the best fats to cook with.

GHEE OR CLARIFIED BUTTER; also high in saturated fat & is actually very good for cooking. You could include butter, but butter has various proteins & sugars which burn at high temperatures so ghee is your best bet as it is pure butter. You can make your own by slowly simmering a block of butter & scraping off the various layers that float to the top.

OILS TO AVOID; the following should not be used for cooking & if they are refined you should probably stay away from them altogether;
     soya bean, canola, sunflower, corn, safflower, rapeseed & sesame oil (toasted).
You can however use the virgin cold pressed of these oils for salads, but not the ones you buy in supermarkets.

Further reading; Udo Erasmus, "Fats that Heal & Fats that Kill". This is the ultimate guide where fats are concerned. I should seriously read this book if you want to explore the fats issue more.

ENZYMES

WHAT IS AN ENZYME?

DEFINITION: A SUBSTANCE PRODUCED BY A LIVING ORGANISM THAT ACTS AS A CATALYST TO BRING ABOUT A SPECIFIC BIOCHEMICAL REACTION.

OR MORE INTERESTINGLY PUT: Enzymes are the workers of the body, there are many & each one has its specific role. They speed up the processes of the body by many billions of times!

Enzymes are needed for practically every process in the body, from digestion, to repair & maintenance work to the body, helping convert calcium into bone, maintaining the immune system; even thinking requires enzyme activity!

There are three main groups of enzymes acting in our bodies; metabolic enzymes (responsible for maintaining the immune system & a wide range of bodily processes), digestive enzymes for digestion & exogenous enzymes, the enzymes we eat through raw foods that pre-digests food for us.

THE FORMER TWO GROUPS OF ENZYMES ARE PRODUCED BY THE BODY. We come equipped with a finite number of enzymes at birth; like a bank account full of money we have to manage these reserves carefully & responsibly, if not the money runs out. How we use our enzymes is fundamentally important to leading a healthy disease free life, just in the same way how we withdraw money from our bank account has a bearing on how much we will have to spend later on.

Dr Edward Howell, who was the pioneer in enzyme research, first came up with "the law of adaptive secretion", in his book, Enzyme Nutrition (Howell, 1985), which states that the body will withdraw enzymes only as & when is needed.

ENZYMES START TO DIE AT 40°C – 105°F & with a large percentage of the global population eating cooked food, the pancreas would be under a lot of strain to produce the necessary digestive enzymes to keep the digestive processes going. This leaves little opportunity for the metabolic enzymes to carry out the necessary repair & maintenance work around the body & eventually, together with the unhealthy life styles, we live we open ourselves up to all sorts of potential trouble later on in life.

All too often we are totally unaware of what is going on the inside of our bodies & too preoccupied with what is going on the outside!

Just like a bank account we need to make deposits of enzymes in our bodies.

SPROUTING

WHEN A SPROUT IS AROUND 1 INCH TALL, IT PACKS MORE NUTRIENTS & ENERGY THAN THE FULLY GROWN VEGETABLE

IMAGINE HOW GOOD IT IS FOR YOU when you eat a handful! It is a really cheap way of getting minerals, antioxidants, vitamins, chlorophyll & enzymes in your body without it being time consuming & this is what you need to do to achieve this:

- put 3 teaspoons of seeds of your choice in a wide necked jar & cover with double the amount of water.

- Cover the top with a mesh or muslin cloth & secure with an elastic band & soak (please see table for soak times).

- After soaking turn the jar round & drain, fill with water & drain again & leave at a 45 degree angle. This allows the water to drain completely & oxygen to circulate inside.

- Every 12 to 16 hours you will need to rinse the seeds by filling the jar with water & drain to keep them moist.

Depending on the seed variety you will see some sprouting action after 1 to 3 days & this is the most important & time consuming part: as the seeds germinate they will discard their husk. These need to be extracted by scooping them out with your hand. When you rinse with water the loose husks will usually stick to one side of the jar when you drain the water & are easily removed. This will prevent any potential rotting of the husk as they are designed to rot back into the earth in nature.

If the seeds start to smell like ammonia, throw them away & start again. It is ok, don't worry it happens from time to time.
Voila! Fresh sprouts in less than 1 minute per day! It really is cheap & definitely not time consuming.

Ikea do good jars for sprouting just make sure the neck is wide enough so you can get your hand in!
A "Sproutman" sprouting bag is very useful for sprouting legumes & beans; you can buy these from www.wholisticresearch.com.
You soak the seeds as per the table, then you keep them in the bag & dunk in water the bag every day, until the sprout is about the same length of the seed itself. Voila!
So that is the more complicated way to Sprout, here is an easier way!

A Chinese steamer (with a mesh) is a great way to sprout. After having soaked the seeds for the required time then you spread the seeds out on the mesh & spray every 8-10 hours with a good quantity of water, for me this is the easiest way. The sprouters you buy these days don't do the job so well as there is always water left behind & therefore you increase your chances of rotting. These dim sum steamer baskets stack up & really don't take much space. You can sprout everything in these! To separate the husk from the seedlings you can buy salad spinners with small holes in the basket, the brand OXO do a mini herb & sprout spinner which works really well.

BELOW IS THE SPROUTING CHART WITH SOAK TIMES

Please note, where I have written husk removed: these do not grow into greens, but are used for pates or can be eaten sprouted. You can put these in a dehydrator at 40 degrees, season & have a raw sprouted snack. Or you can blitz the sprouted seeds once dehydrated & use as a raw flour to make bases for raw crackers & breads.

The husk (protective jacket of the seed) is there for a reason, as protection so that the seed will grow strong. If you try & sprout the same seed without the husk then it won't grow the same, these seeds are used for different recipes. Everything you need from: www.wheatgrass-uk.com & www.wholisticresearch.com

SOAKING & SPROUTING TABLE

SEED	SOAK TIME	SPROUTING TIME
All Nuts	12 hours	these nuts will be used for milks
Except peanuts		
Sunflower (husk removed) pates &	4 hours	12-24 hours (not for greens) for cheeses
Pumpkin (husk removed)	4 hours	12-24 hours (not for greens)
Buckwheat (husk removed)	1-4 hours	12-24 hours (not for greens)
Lentils	12 hours	3 days
Chickpeas	12 hours	3 days
Adzuki beans	12 hours	4 days
Mung	12 hours	3 days
Wheat (husk removed)	6 hours	2 days (not for greens)
Kamut (husk removed)	6 hours	2 days (not for greens)
Spelt	6 hours	2 days (not for greens)
Rye	6 hours	2 days (not for greens)
Barley	6 hours	2 days (not for greens)
Quinoa	4-6 hours	24 hours
Alfalfa	6 hours	5 days
Clover	6 hours	5 days
Fenugreek	8-12 hours	5 days

BLOOD PH

BLOOD PH. PH. IS A MEASURE OF HOW ACIDIC OR ALKALINE SOMETHING IS

BELOW 7 IS ACIDIC & ABOVE IS ALKALINE. Our blood is designed to be in-between 7.3 & 7.4, slightly alkaline. Dr William Hay observed that the more acidic his patients' blood was the less well they were & the more toxic their blood was.

THESE DAYS OUR DIETS ARE VERY ACIDIFYING for the blood: coffee, alcohol, black tea, meat, fish, ALL dairy, breads using refined white flour. (Please see what I agree to be the definitive list of alkalising & acidifying foods, by Ross Bridgeford from www. energiseforlife.com) Thank you Ross.

THERE ARE TESTS ONE CAN DO: testing saliva & urine, but these have to be done over longer periods & can be inaccurate. Urine & saliva are slightly acidic & the ph will vary depending on what time of day it is. Furthermore we are not testing the acidity of a food but we are seeing what that food does to your blood ph AFTER it is digested. Some methods for testing burn the food & then test the ashes. We need to see what the food does after it is digested. For example a lemon is acidic, but it is alkalising for the body, the same goes for apple cider vinegar. So the only accurate test in my view is a blood test.

USUALLY THE MORE SUGAR something has in it the more acidic it is for the body, a fresh apple is less acidifying than a dried one where the natural sugars are concentrated. This is why a lemon is alkalising, no sugar content.
Generally speaking we need an 80/20 ratio of alkalising to acidifying food. Today it looks more like 20/80! Have a look at the chart & see where you fit in to all this.
When testing the blood, anything below PH 7 needs correcting, a rapid alkalisation can be achieved by doing a juice fast.

IN CASES OF UNUSUALLY HIGH ACID LEVELS, this may prevent your organs from getting the amount of oxygen they need. As a result, your muscles may be weak, or you may not have the energy you need to sustain you throughout the day. Headaches & fatigue may make it difficult for you to concentrate or remain attentive while carrying out your daily activities.

GROWING YOUR OWN GREENS

THIS IS REALLY EASY, you will need: some gravel trays with no holes in the bottom, so you don't drip everywhere indoors, organic compost & earth, a cup of wheatgrass or Spelt seeds with the husk on, a watering can & a sprouting bag/jar or a Chinese dim sum steamer. You need to follow the previous instructions for sprouting (the sprout bag is good for this seed) & when the sprout is the same length as the seed, it is time to plant. Fill the gravel tray up with a 50/50 ratio of compost & hummus & then spread the seeds so they cover the earth on top. Then a tiny sprinkling of water & cover the tray with another tray upside down to create a greenhouse (the seed will water themselves as they will produce water when they breathe). Seeds do not need light to germinate, think of nature & how they sprout... Underground! Then leave for 4 days with the top on, no peeking! You will see the new shoots pushing up the top tray. Time to take the lid off & allow the plant to create chlorophyll via photosynthesis, a stunning process where the plant draws up the inorganic minerals form the earth & turns them into organic bio available minerals for us! That goes for all plants

Wheatgrass (with husk)	12 hours	7-10 days for wheatgrass juice
Sunflower (with husk)	12 hours	7-10 days for salad greens
Snow Pea (with husk)	24 hours	7-10 days for salad greens
Buckwheat (with husk)	12 hours	7-10 days for salad greens

CHLOROPHYLL & WHEATGRASS

Chlorophyll is formed in plants by photosynthesis. This enables the plant to convert inorganic minerals into organic ones which are readily absorbed by the body. It also has a very similar chemical formula to the "Haem" part of haemoglobin, please see diagram.

I won't go on too much about this, read either the "Wheatgrass Book", by Anne Wigmore, or "Lliving Foods for Radiant Health", by Elaine Bruce, (my tutor). They are both great books!

THERE ARE OVER 90 MINERALS IN WHEATGRASS JUICE

& it is over 70 % chlorophyll. All of the essential amino acids are present & so it has been described as a first class protein, or a complete food. The word essential indicates our bodies cannot produce them so we have to eat them daily for our bodies to function. There is typically 2.8% protein in wheatgrass & all the B vitamins including, B17 (amygdalin). B17 has been called the "cancer killer" & it has done away with many cancers, there are many success stories from the likes of "The Gerson Clinic" & the "Hippocrates Institute" & countless books on the subject.

But once again, beware this can only work in conjunction with a lifestyle change, you cannot pretend you will heal by just having a shot of wheatgrass a day & having 12 gin & tonics, 1 pack of cigarettes & a deep pan pizza! But for more on this subject check out the above mentioned books. Elaine Bruce & Anne Wigmore have come up with great programmes that you can follow at home. But remember you have to want it, not want to want it!

Now a list of how chlorophyll can help you:
- ॐ It purifies/cleanses & builds blood
- ॐ Produces an unfriendly environment for bad bacteria
- ॐ Builds & regenerates cells
- ॐ Is a great vitamin, mineral & enzyme supplement.

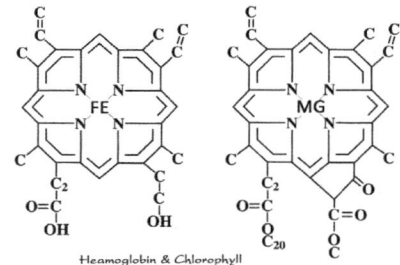

Heamoglobin & Chlorophyll

HELPS WITH WEIGHT REGULATION, the body's message to the stomach is not a "fill me up with something now" message, but an "I need nutrients" message. I have done this at home, drinking a shot of wheatgrass & my hunger has gone away for a few hours.

Taken rectally it repopulates the good flora & is absorbed immediately. After an enema you need to repopulate your colon with good bacteria. This is one way of doing it; the other is taking a live pro-biotic supplement.

Recently my friend came out in a bad rash on her chest & applied wheat grass juice to the problem area, the next day it was gone. This works really well applied topically on cuts, rashes, spots and it has even helped mild eczema.

It helps cure dandruff. You can also use as an eye wash & nasal decongestant.

It is great at removing toxins, especially heavy metals, it is a good idea to have a proper detox however as we are all quite toxic. For detoxes see www.detoxinternational.com

Note; if you have amalgam fillings drink wheatgrass with a straw as it can break down the mercury.

THIS INDEED IS LIQUID SUNSHINE, life force; think about it, grass came to the earth 60 million years ago. Why is it everywhere? To feed the masses of animals that eat it! Protein: be aware that the protein content in wheatgrass juice comes nowhere near the necessary amount your body needs per day.

NO TIME TO EAT PROPERLY?
LET'S CHEAT!

Life is such that we often don't have time to eat healthy, myself included!

Supplements are exactly what they say on the bottle, they are never to be taken in the place of a healthy diet. I am so busy here during the season that I have no time to eat, nor do I feel like it. Working in a kitchen for 10 hours a day really suppresses my appetite, unless Tracey fixes us some new delights!

This is merely a list of what "I" do & in no way is a prescription of any sort, or in the place of professional medical advice. This is maintenance for me, tried & tested by me & it works for ME.

Getting up, I have a nice cup of coffee; followed by a cup or 2 of hot water & lemon (with grated ginger) this goes some way to neutralising the large acidifying effect of the coffee.

I have 1 cayenne capsule every day; simply read the home remedies part on Cayenne for its benefits. You can buy these from Amazon (the best brand is Solgar for these), or buy your own empty capsules & fill then yourself. If you have inflammation you can make your own turmeric capsules for example:

I have 500 ml of a freeze dried green drink, an all in one enzyme, mineral & vitamin drink (this is instead of a freshly squeezed juice) the brand Kiki for me is the best as it is 100% raw & also there are no "fillers" as there are with other brands, it is expensive but worth it. When I grow & juice my own wheatgrass, I don't have the powdered drink. Plus every time I have a cooked meal I take one of Udo's enzyme blends, to take the pressure off my digestive system.

ॐ 1 teaspoon of raw chocolate, this has one of the highest levels of antioxidants & rich in iron. There is a massive discussion about this, detrimental or not? Some raw foodies say have as much as you can eat, I disagree, & there are things in raw chocolate that CAN be detrimental to us if you eat loads of it. Personally there is nothing wrong with having a teaspoon on your muesli in the morning.

ॐ 1 teaspoon of raw organic honey, great for internal healing, the Moroccans use this as a medicine on a daily basis, when within their means!

ॐ 1 teaspoon of organic molasses, over 50 different minerals, the good part of the sugar.

ॐ a hand full of almonds, walnuts, sunflower & pumpkin seeds.

ॐ a couple of teaspoons of shelled hemp, a great source of protein & omega 3 & 6 fatty acids.

ॐ a hand full of goji berries (always organic there are some dubious non organic ones around).

ॐ 3 brazil nuts a day, contains your daily portion of Selenium, an antioxidant.

If I want a glass of milk I have Almond milk. In a liquid state everything is so much more bio available to us, than when we have to chew. I also have a teaspoon of coconut butter a day. Great for hair, nails skin & has loads of antioxidants. For a constipation free life, I soak some chia & linseed & add to my muesli or just eat as is. Try & chew the seeds too to release the excellent omega fatty acids within. I have all this in front of me & pick all day. Best of all, next time you are getting a low on energy & falling asleep at your desk, instead of reaching for the coffee, down 400 ml of water! If you can eat healthily on top of that & juice every day that's great! If not then At least you are doing something for your body in the way of nutrition.

Sometimes I take 2 drops of 35% hydrogen peroxide solution in a glass of water for a week or two.

Yes the 35% is dangerous when drunk "neat", all our cells produce it as a first line of defence when we get raided by bacteria or viruses. Before using this however, I recommend you read Conrad Lebeau's book on the subject, it makes for very interesting reading. I know what you are thinking, that's the solution to bleach hair, yes indeed it is but it is the concentration that counts. Happy reading.

There are six naturopathic principles I try & live by. These words sound commonplace but systems of medicine have been built around them (not Western medicine obviously).

ॐ Variety   ॐ Simplicity   ॐ Balance
ॐ Moderation   ॐ Harmony   ॐ Cooperation (with your body)

Honey **IS** sugar, & it is loaded with calories (good calories), which is why I only have a teaspoon per day. If you start using honey for everything from cooking to preparing food then you will put on weight. MODERATION!

MILKS (WHEN WE SAY MILK WE MEAN COMMERCIALLY PRODUCED COW'S MILK & ITS DERIVATIVES)

We try to stay away from commercially produced cow's milk here at the centre. Contrary to popular belief cow's milk & its derivatives are NOT good for you, yes it has calcium, but it does not get absorbed by the body the way it should.

Why? Because when milk reaches the super market it is so acidifying for the body that it will actually deplete your calcium reserves to neutralise the acidity of the milk. If you do like a drop of milk in your coffee then fine, the body can handle that but please don't believe it is good for you just because people & companies say so, it is really not the case.

Cow's milk also contains potentially harmful levels of both synthetic hormone residues & antibiotic residues from commercial high intensity dairy farming: plus it contains natural growth hormones meant for the baby calves, NOT you!

You need about 1000mg of calcium per day (the equivalent of 1 glass of milk plus a yogurt).

Here is a list of non-dairy foods that contain more than enough of your calcium needs in one day: Almonds (10 nuts gives you around 120mg of calcium), all dark leafy greens, broccoli, tofu 100g gives you 350mg of Calcium (must be organic to avoid GMO), sesame seeds (try a tahini)100g of sesame seeds gives 975mg of calcium, dried green herbs (contain around 100mg per teaspoon), linseeds (flax), Brazil nuts, & the list goes on.

Well I guess what I am trying to say here is that if you eat a varied diet then you will have all the calcium you need in a day without relying on dairy. And it will be in a bio available format, unlike conventional cow's milk. I am not saying give dairy up, but you do have an option if you are vegan, or if you are thinking of giving dairy up.

FERMENTATION

Simply put, there are good bacteria (eating fermented foods), & bad bacteria, (when the food ferments inside your body), unfortunately most of the time we have the bad variety. Usually this is caused by the improper digestion of food in your system & this happens because we combine the wrong foods at the same time, not chewing correctly & also drinking water during the meal contributes to the fermentation you do not want.

So, what is really going on? We have different digestive enzymes for carbs & proteins & because we don't eat enough exogenous enzymes our bodies are always struggling to digest the food we don't chew properly.

Basically the 2 enzyme groups get confused & subsequently you have food which is not properly digested. This undigested food starts to ferment & it is this fermentation that is causing the bad bacteria in your gut. The same happens when food is not chewed properly; remember your granny saying chew at least 30 times? Well she was right. Food needs to really resemble something which has been put through a blender, this gives the enzymes half a chance to digest it, especially when it is not raw & does not have its own living enzymes. There is one way of seeing if you have enough good bacteria; when you go to the bathroom, if it floats then you do, if it doesn't you need a probiotic.

Here is what you can do for natural probiotics:

Sauerkraut, you can buy organic one or make it very cheaply yourself:
Take a cabbage & slice it thinly & in a metal or plastic bowl, bash with the end of a rolling pin until the juices release. Put everything in a wide-necked jar & fill with water until all the cabbage is under water. Fill a tumbler with water & place in the jar so it compresses the cabbage, add whatever flavouring you like: garlic, chilli, rosemary etc. & wait for 4 days, there will be lots of bubbles as the bacteria does its work. Keep in the fridge, this lasts for a long time. If it smells off then time to throw it away & start a new batch.

Fermented water; this uses "water grains" that you can buy from www.kefirshop.co.uk
This is prepared using water & brown sugar for the bacteria's food.

Kefir (dairy) this is made with milk, goat or cow, the bacteria eat the lactose.
This uses kefir grains, which you can buy. You can buy kefir drink from any Moroccan shop.
www.kefirshop.co.uk

A little note: Goats milk is only slightly acidifying whereas cow's milk is very acidifying for the body.

Tamari sauce (gluten free soy sauce, always check the label!) & miso paste sauce.
These are both fermented; why not use them for salad dressings?

And if you do have a heavy cooked meal, to help digestion, get Udo's enzyme blend & take one during your meal, your body will then not need to expend so much energy to digest.
www.udoschoice.co.uk/

SUGARS & OTHER SWEET MEDIUMS

ASPARTAME: This is the most common artificial sweetener (E951) which "reportedly" is a neuron toxin which we recommend you avoid! A huge amount of processed products, including most diet products contain artificial sweetener (aspartame) along with; soft drinks, cookies, breakfast cereals, & even some children's vitamin supplements!

There are many sweeteners & sugars out there & this can prove a little bit of a mine field. Sugars should really be in the same category as bad fats, they are just as much a killer. Also they are EVREYWHERE! A bit of natural sugar from a piece of fresh fruit is fine for example: it is "stealth" sugars that we need to worry about. The syrups & low grade forms of fructose that are added in a lot of processed foods are the killers; we often eat them without knowing, such as low fat yogurts. Yes they have no fat but you will usually find sugar in these. "No fat", in our minds makes us think of "No weight gain", but it is really not the case. Sugar interferes with insulin function, damages teeth, feeds bacteria, yeast, fungus, & cancer cells. It also pulls calcium & other minerals from the body.

IN SUMMARY, HIGH FAT DIETS CAUSE HEALTH PROBLEMS: diets deficient in essential fats, cause health problems: & sugars cause health problems, good grief! What's left to eat?

We hardly use any sugar here in the book, except for a few desserts, & when possible we use date paste. We have experimented by trying to create date sugar by putting the dates in an oven on a medium heat for a longish time, careful because they are very easy to burn. The trick is to cut the dates into quarters, otherwise the edges burn before the centre becomes crystallised. Once they go dark brown allow to dry, the sugars will then crystallise, ready for the processor..... Voila, date sugar!!

RAW ORGANIC DARK SUGARCANE is what I often use. I buy this from my local organic farmers market, its fair trade!

XYLITOL is good. It is made from the bark of the Birch Tree & is present in other fruit & veg. It is quite expensive though.

STEVIA is from a herb but it does taste a little of aniseed though. We tried to bake a cake with it once. We were not entirely convinced. We used the herb itself, although there are other forms of processed Stevia which resemble sugar.

AGAVE SYRUP: please do not believe anyone who says it is good for you; it is after all a highly processed refined food which has been heat treated & has more fructose than the dreaded corn syrup!
We use it in only a couple of our recipes & in very little quantity.

RAW ORGANIC HONEY: a great sugar with the usual host of benefits that it brings. There are also curative properties, check it in Conrad Lebeau's book of natural Home Remedies.

ORGANIC MAPLE SYRUP: (one of my favourites), another substitute for processed sugar which is also suitable for vegans.

If you are serious about a "living food diet", I would highly recommend investing in a professional dehydrator (such as the fore mentioned Excalibur). As sun or air-drying, can be somewhat hit or miss when it comes to regulating the temperature. A dehydrator is pretty much invaluable in damp or humid climates.

However there are a couple of other options... For those of you who happen to live in sunny climates, or those of you who have a log burner installed in your home. The main objective is to keep warm & dry, & also to obtain air circulation, if only at a minimum.

MY SUMMER METHOD is to sun-dry either in the garden or in the car
Line a metal tray with aluminium & place your produce cut side up (if drying cut tomato halves for example). Leaving a small gap between each piece of fruit & veg.
You can place them in the sun, just make sure that you secure a piece of mosquito netting, or a fly cover, to prevent the bugs from laying eggs inside your snacks! I use adhesive tape to secure mine to the base of the tray, ensuring bug control.
However, you should be aware of the humid night air; I take my frames in every evening & place them out on my terrace again the next morning.
You can avoid this daily route end by placing the tray in your car. This keeps the damp off your produce. However open the windows just enough so that the air can circulate, just a centimetre is enough.
If you live in a hot climate, there are various options & instructions on-line to build your own solar dehydrator; some are built using recycled materials!
MY WINTER METHOD is to dehydrate using the heat created by my log burner.
We have wooden shelves in our kitchen, which run above the log burner. My husband Steve also made a "Dolly". An old fashioned wooden device that hangs from our kitchen ceiling, it's elevated by pulling on a rope, also used for drying our laundry, perfect for dehydrating!

Place your sliced produce on either a fly screen (I use one that is mounted in an aluminium **frame** for easy cleaning). Or simply place produce on a piece of cardboard covered in a non-stick parchment paper, either on a warm shelf, or a dolly. This system will however take a little longer, as the air cannot pass so freely.
Check the progress every four to six hours.
Some produce such as herbs, or flowers only take a few hours to dry in a warm environment, so check them regularly. Sliced apples or kale will dehydrate faster than fruits that are composed of a lot of water, such as strawberries or melon. The length of time will also depend on the temperature, air circulation, along with the thickness & the type of fruit or veg you are drying.

Basic natural dehydration methods. These times appear random, as they are only estimated drying guidelines from my experience eco-drying in either the sun or over my log burner. Not in a dedicated dehydration unit!

To obtain a leathery texture naturally:		To obtain a crisp texture	
Tomato halves	3-5 days	Broccoli	10-20 hrs
Apple slices	8-24 hrs	Kale or cabbage	8-12 hrs
Guava sliced	5-12 hrs	Courgette	6-12 hrs

LINKS & FURTHER READING
(UK & USA SITES)

All you need for living foods, Juicers, seeds sprouters, very professional people who actually answer the phone & help when you call!
UK: www.wholisticresearch.com   USA: www.sproutpeople.org

Thermomix for info worldwide visit
www.thermomix.com

Great guides for home remedies & prevention, you can read these books in a couple of hours
UK: www.lebeaubooks.com

Elaine Bruce's website for all that is living foods
UK: www.livingfoods.co.uk

Sells kefir grains for dairy & water.
UK: www.kefirshop.co.uk   USA: www.kefirlady.com

For good fats/bad fats guide & products
UK: www.udoschoice.co.uk   USA: www.udoerasmus.com

For all your seeds you need for sprouting
UK: www.wheatgrass-uk.com   USA: www.wheatgrasskits.com

Type in any spice or herb in the search box & review case studies
www.herballegacy.com   USA: www.mountainroseherbs.com
Our great friend Midi Fairgrieve website for detox retreats.
www.detox-international.com

The Gerson institute is for Cancer sufferers who are looking for an alternative natural treatment.
www.gerson.org

A fantastic website with loads of case studies, this is the website that tells an amazing story of using Cayenne pepper to fight ulcers!
www.herballegacy.com   USA: www.homeremediesandtreatments.com

Our friend in Texas has a family run business; they produce "Chili Hellion" Smoked Habanero Powder
Natural habanero peppers, slow smoked in a wood-fired pit by his grandfather!
It's amazing, I eat it with everything! Add it to your carrot cake, soup, or sprinkle over salad.
www.chilihellion.com

"Zeolite" is a product which helps take toxins away from your body.
www.alphaclear.com

A

ALMONDS
almond milk & cream 112
ajo blanco 25
amalou 42
cauliflower & almond soup 27
raw almond butter 50
couscous feta & almonds 86
orange & almond cake 104
walnut & sesame halva 105

AUBERGINES (EGG-PLANT)
roast aubergine salad 32
stuffed aubergine 89

AVOCADOS
alkalizing avocado halves 38
avocado & peach dip 50
chocolate mousse 97
chocolate cheesecake 101
ensalada la mota 37
key lime pie 100

B

BASIL
pesto 53

BBQ SAUCE (see MARINADES)

BEAN-CURD (see TOFU)

BEANS & PULSES
broad bean dip 47
chili sin carne 90
sprouting 121
coconut & lentil dhal 77
Soy beans (see SOYA)

BEETROOT
beetroot gazpacho 26
bread 56
ensalada la mota 37
raw tortilla wraps 67
spiralized spaghetti 81
sprouted lentil salad 31

BREAD 56

BROCOLI
sprouted quinoa salad 33

BURGERS
Britti's Burgers 75

C

Cajun Rub 49

CARROTS
carrot salad 36
carrot, date & ginger cake 105

CAULIFLOWER
cauliflower & almond soup 27
indian curry 77

CHEESE
cheesy sun-dried tomato scones 57
spinach & feta muffins 60
vegan cheese with herbs 48

CHICKPEAS (Garbanzos see BEANS)

CHOCOLATE
chocolate mousse 97
choco cranberry slab 97
chocolate cheesecake 101
choco sunshine paste 104

CHILLIE
chili sin carne 90
fresh green chili harissa 50

COCONUT
african coconut curry 69
choco cranberry slab 97
coconut & lentil dhal 77
indian curry 77
spanking good pancakes 59

CORN (MAIZ)
corn fritters 59

CRACKRS
raw flax &chia crackers 64
garlic & parmesan crackers 64

COURGETTES (Zucchini)
Pad Thai 34
Roasted Courgette, Pear,
Walnut & Feta Salad 35
Courgette Hummus 41
Raw tortilla wraps 67
Courgette Lasagna 72
Roast veg 78
Creamy Tomato Pasta Sauce with
spiralized spaghetti 81

COUSCOUS
couscous, feta & Almonds 86

CURRY
roasted curry powder 47
african Curry 69
indian Curry 77

D

DATES
fresh green chili harissa 50
date paste 97
chocolate mousse 97
carrot, date & ginger cake 105
walnut & sesame halva 105
creamy pasta sauce 81

DIPS
avocado & peach dip 50
broad bean 47
chive & garlic 52
jerk 45
roasted pepper & cashew 47
salsa verde 52

DONUTS 67

DRESSINGS 39

E

EGG-PLANT (see AUBERGINES)

F

fajitas 90
falafel 74

FRUIT (see individual fruits)

G

GARLIC
Ajo Blanco (see gazpacho)
Gem hearts with fried garlic 33

GAZPACHOS (cold soups)
melon, avocado & mint 23
Richi's Gazpacho 23
Pineapple 25
watermelon 24
beetroot 26
ajo blanco 25

GRAINS
Living Muesli 58

NOTES

NOTES

We want you to be inspired & creative,
but above all, we want you to have fun with this book!
Our aim is to make vegetarian, vegan, raw
& gluten-free diets easy going, with
lip-smacking recipes!

This book is designed to help you achieve a
level of good health & energy without having to
take large daunting steps, or eating tasteless foods.

We look at all different types of food,
from raw to roasted to sprouting, from different
parts of the world & what these foods can do
for you on a nutritional level.
There is something for everybody in this book
& we hope you enjoy the recipes,
information & the tips within.

Richard & Tracey

Printed in Great Britain
by Amazon.co.uk, Ltd.,
Marston Gate.